FIREFIGHTER EXAM PREP

A STEP-BY-STEP GUIDE TO ACE THE TEST ON YOUR FIRST TRY | COMPLETE WITH 400+ Q&A PLUS A 30-DAY STUDY PLAN TO ENSURE YOUR SUCCESS WITH CONFIDENCE

DANIEL GILDER

Copyright © 2024 by Daniel Gilder

All rights reserved. No part of this publication may be reproduced, distributed, or transmitted in any form or by any means, including photocopying, recording, or other electronic or mechanical methods, without the prior written permission of the publisher, except in the case of brief quotations embodied in critical reviews and certain other noncommercial uses permitted by copyright law. For permission requests, write to the publisher, addressed "Attention: Permissions Coordinator," at the address below.

TABLE OF CONTENTS

INTRODUCTION 9
   Your Roadmap: How This Book Will Guide You to Success 9
   The Firefighter's Mindset: Preparing Mentally for Your Career 11
   Embarking on the Journey: Understanding the Firefighter Exam 13
   Structure of the Exam and Expectations 15
   State-by-State Variations: Adapting to Regional Requirements 17

CHAPTER 1 21
CONQUERING READING COMPREHENSION 21
   The importance of reading comprehension in firefighting 21
   Overview of the exam segment. 23
   Critical Reading Strategies 25
      Techniques for skimming and scanning 25
      In-depth reading vs. surface reading: When and how to apply each .. 27
   Tackling Different Question Types 29
      Direct questions: Finding explicit answers 29
      Inference questions: Deriving implicit meanings 31
      Vocabulary and context analysis. 33

CHAPTER 2 39
MASTERING MATHEMATICAL REASONING 39
   The Quantitative Edge 39
      The role of math in firefighting 39
      Overview of the mathematical reasoning section 41
   Essential Mathematical Concepts 43
      Basic arithmetic and algebra 43
      Geometry and statistics basics for firefighters 45

Problem-Solving Techniques 47
  Step-by-step approaches to solving typical exam problems 47
  Common mathematical traps and how to avoid them. 49

CHAPTER 3 53
MECHANICAL REASONING UNLOCKED 53

Mechanics in Firefighting 53
  The importance of mechanical reasoning. 53
  Overview of the Mechanical Reasoning section 55

Principles of Mechanics 57
  Levers, pulleys, gears, and inclined planes 57
  Understanding force and torque 59

Mechanical Aptitude in Action 61
  Real-world applications in firefighting equipment and scenarios 61
  Approaching and solving mechanical reasoning questions 63

CHAPTER 4 67
NAVIGATING SITUATIONAL JUDGMENT 67

Decision-Making Under Pressure 67
  The significance of situational judgment for firefighters 67
  Exam format and types of scenarios presented. 69

Understanding Situational Judgment 71
  Framework for effective decision-making 71
  Analyzing the situation: What you need to consider 73

Responding to Emergencies 75
  Prioritizing actions under time constraints 75
  Explanation of ideal responses and common mistakes 77

CHAPTER 5 83

SPATIAL ORIENTATION EXPERTISE 83
  Mapping Success 83
    The role of spatial awareness in firefighting. 83
    Overview of the spatial orientation section. 85
  Fundamental Concepts of Spatial Orientation 87
    Understanding maps, diagrams, and spatial relationships 87
  Visual and Spatial Problem Solving 89
    Strategies for tackling orientation and visualization questions 89
    Tips for interpreting and navigating through complex layouts 91

CHAPTER 6 95
PRACTICAL QUESTIONS AND ANSWERS 95
  Reading Comprehension Practical Questions 95
  MATHEMATICAL REASONING PRACTICAL QUESTIONS 108
  MECHANICAL REASONING PRACTICAL QUESTIONS 117
  SITUATIONAL JUDGMENT PRACTICAL QUESTIONS 127
  SPATIAL ORIENTATION PRACTICAL QUESTIONS 142
  READING COMPREHENSION ANSWER KEY 153
  MATHEMATICAL REASONING ANSWER KEY 161
  MECHANICAL REASONING ANSWER KEY 167
  SITUATIONAL JUDGMENT ANSWER KEY 175
  SPATIAL ORIENTATION ANSWER KEY 186

CHAPTER 7 193
BONUS 193
  30-Day Study Plan: Your Daily Prep Guide 193
  Test Day Strategies: Peak Performance When It Counts 197
  Physical Test Tips: Preparing Your Body for the Challenge 199

Managing Stress Before, During, and After the Exam 201
Career Path and Advancement Advice 203
CONCLUSION 205
Encouragement to embrace the challenges and rewards of a firefighting career 205

INTRODUCTION

Your Roadmap: How This Book Will Guide You to Success

Embarking on the journey to become a firefighter is no small feat; it requires not only physical strength and agility but also a sharp, well-prepared mind. This book is crafted with the understanding that each candidate possesses the potential to excel, provided they have the right tools and guidance. Thus, "Firefighter Exam Prep: A Step-by-Step Guide to Ace the Test on Your First Try" is designed not just as a study manual but as a comprehensive navigator through the intricate landscape of firefighter exam preparation.

From the outset, this guide is structured to build your knowledge progressively, ensuring that no stone is left unturned. We begin by setting a solid foundation of what to expect on the exam, detailing the various components and the type of content that will be encountered. This is crucial as it helps demystify the exam process, making it less daunting and more approachable. By understanding the structure of the exam and the expectations set forth, you can tailor your study approach effectively, focusing on areas that demand more attention while consolidating those you are already comfortable with.

As you delve deeper into the book, you'll find each chapter dedicated to a specific section of the exam—Reading Comprehension, Mathematical Reasoning, Mechanical Reasoning, Situational Judgment, and Spatial Orientation. Each of these sections is pivotal in assessing the diverse skills required in firefighting. Reading Comprehension, for instance, is not merely about understanding words on a page but grasping the critical information, making inferences, and applying this understanding to real-world firefighting scenarios. Similarly, Mathematical Reasoning goes beyond simple calculations; it involves applying mathematical concepts to solve problems effectively, a skill indispensable in the field where quick and accurate decisions can save lives.

Moreover, Mechanical Reasoning is introduced with detailed explanations of mechanical principles such as levers, pulleys, and gears, which are not only part of the exam but are also integral to firefighting operations. Understanding how these mechanisms work underpins a firefighter's ability to manipulate equipment and tools in emergency situations. Furthermore, the Situational Judgment tests your ability to make quick, effective decisions in high-pressure scenarios, mirroring the real-life decisions firefighters make every day.

Spatial Orientation, another critical section, tests your ability to navigate and make decisions in physical spaces, an undeniable necessity in the chaotic environments firefighters often find themselves in. The book offers strategies and practice questions to enhance your spatial reasoning skills, ensuring you can confidently handle this part of the exam.

The journey through the book is supplemented with practice questions that mirror the actual test, allowing you to test your knowledge as you progress. These questions not only reinforce the material covered but also familiarize you with the exam format and question types. This dual approach of learning and practicing is a cornerstone of effective exam preparation and is emphasized throughout the guide.

To ensure no aspect of your preparation is overlooked, the book concludes with a bonus chapter that encompasses a 30-day study plan, test day strategies, and tips for physical readiness. This holistic approach ensures that you are not only mentally but also physically prepared to take on the challenges of the exam and the demands of a firefighting career.

In crafting this guide, the goal has been clear: to provide a pathway to success that is as informative as it is empowering. By the end of this book, you should feel not just prepared but confident in your ability to ace the firefighter exam on your first try. The book doesn't just prepare you for an exam; it prepares you for a career, equipping you with knowledge, strategies, and insights that will serve you well beyond the test day. Through this detailed roadmap, the hope is to not only see you succeed in passing the exam but also in embarking on a rewarding and impactful career in firefighting.

The Firefighter's Mindset: Preparing Mentally for Your Career

Embarking on a career as a firefighter requires more than physical prowess; it demands a robust mental framework capable of handling intense pressure, critical decision-making, and emotional resilience. This chapter delves into the psychological fortitude necessary not only to pass the firefighter exam but also to excel in a demanding and often perilous profession. Understanding and developing the right mindset is crucial for those who aspire to enter this noble and challenging field.

The journey begins with cultivating a mindset of service and sacrifice. Firefighting is not just a job; it is a commitment to protecting and serving the community in times of dire need. This calling requires a deep-seated desire to help others, often at one's own risk. It's about running toward danger when everyone else is running away. Thus, a firefighter must develop an altruistic spirit, placing the well-being of others above personal safety. This sense of duty is what drives firefighters to perform with courage and dedication, even under the most stressful conditions.

Resilience is another cornerstone of the firefighter's mental makeup. The nature of firefighting can be unforgiving, with exposure to life-threatening situations, devastating fires, and, at times, the heartbreak of loss. Mental resilience helps firefighters recover from these hardships and continue to perform their duties effectively. Building this resilience involves regular mental health practices such as mindfulness and meditation, as well as seeking support from peers and professionals. These practices help mitigate the effects of stress and trauma, ensuring that firefighters remain mentally sharp and emotionally stable.

Moreover, mental preparedness for the firefighter exam and the job goes beyond handling emotional stress; it also encompasses intellectual readiness. Firefighting requires a broad knowledge base, from understanding fire behavior and building construction to knowing medical procedures and hazardous material management. Preparing to pass the firefighter exam, therefore, involves rigorous study and comprehension of diverse subjects that are all applicable to the scenarios they will face on the job.

Critical thinking and problem-solving are vital skills in this regard. On the fireground, every second counts, and the ability to quickly analyze a situation and make informed decisions can mean the difference between life and death. This level of proficiency is achieved through scenario-based training and simulations that mimic real-life emergencies. These exercises train aspiring firefighters to think on their feet, develop situational awareness, and apply their knowledge practically and efficiently.

Adaptability is also essential. The unpredictable nature of emergency calls means that no two situations are the same. A firefighter must be flexible and adaptable, able to modify tactics and strategies at a moment's notice. This adaptability not only applies to physical responses but also to mental strategies, adjusting one's approach to problem-solving as conditions change.

Teamwork cannot be overstated in the context of firefighting. The safety and effectiveness of fire operations depend heavily on the ability to work cohesively as a team. Each team member relies on the others to perform their roles effectively. Developing trust and communication skills is crucial, as these elements foster a strong team dynamic that is essential for the high-stakes nature of firefighting.

Preparation for the firefighter exam is as much about studying textbooks and understanding technical information as it is about preparing mentally for the challenges of the job. This comprehensive approach ensures that candidates are not only ready to pass the exam but are also well-prepared to undertake the responsibilities of a firefighter.

To excel in this career, one must maintain a learner's attitude, constantly seeking new knowledge and skills. The field of firefighting is ever-evolving, with new technologies and techniques continually emerging. A successful firefighter remains curious and informed, always ready to adapt and learn.

Embarking on the Journey: Understanding the Firefighter Exam

Embarking on the journey to become a firefighter, one encounters the initial hurdle, which is the firefighter exam. This exam is more than just a standard test; it is a comprehensive assessment designed to evaluate the readiness of candidates to handle the multifaceted challenges of firefighting. Understanding the structure, purpose, and expectations of this exam is crucial for any aspiring firefighter, as it lays the groundwork for a career that is both demanding and immensely rewarding.

The primary purpose of the firefighter exam is to ensure that all candidates possess the necessary knowledge, skills, and abilities essential for the safe and effective performance of firefighting duties. The nature of firefighting requires a unique blend of physical prowess, cognitive ability, and emotional stability. As such, the exam is meticulously crafted to test these attributes, ensuring that those who pass are well-equipped to take on the rigorous demands of the job.

Structurally, the firefighter exam typically comprises several components, each designed to test different aspects of a candidate's abilities. These include written tests, physical ability tests, medical examinations, and sometimes, psychological evaluations. The written test usually covers topics such as fire science, mechanical reasoning, reading comprehension, mathematical reasoning, and situational judgment. These topics are integral to the daily responsibilities of a firefighter, involving scenarios that require quick, effective decision-making, problem-solving, and a thorough understanding of firefighting techniques and safety protocols.

The physical ability test is another crucial component, assessing a candidate's fitness level and ability to perform physical tasks that are common in firefighting. This might include climbing ladders, carrying heavy equipment, dragging hoses, and rescuing victims, all of which demand not only strength and endurance but also the ability to perform under pressure. This part of the exam is designed to simulate the physical challenges faced during actual fire emergencies, ensuring that candidates can handle the strenuous physical demands of the job.

Additionally, the medical examination confirms that candidates are in good health and free from any medical conditions that could impair their ability to perform firefighting duties. This is vital, as the physical and mental stresses of firefighting can exacerbate underlying health issues. The psychological evaluation, where applicable, aims to assess the mental resilience and emotional stability of the candidates, ensuring they can cope with the high-stress situations and often traumatic scenes they will encounter.

Candidates are expected to arrive at the exam fully prepared, not just academically but physically and mentally. Preparation for the firefighter exam is a rigorous process that involves studying technical materials, undergoing physical training, and cultivating mental resilience. Candidates should have a deep understanding of fire science principles, emergency medical techniques, building codes, hazardous materials, and the mechanics of fire suppression and rescue operations. They should also be familiar with the laws and regulations that govern firefighting activities.

Moreover, candidates are expected to demonstrate a commitment to ethical behavior and integrity, as the role of a firefighter is one of trust and responsibility within the community. This includes a commitment to continuous learning and professional development, as the field of firefighting is continually evolving with new technologies and techniques.

Preparation for the firefighter exam is not just about passing a test; it's about proving oneself capable of handling a career that can be both physically exhausting and emotionally draining. It requires a combination of theoretical knowledge and practical skills that are only honed through dedication and hard work.

Structure of the Exam and Expectations

The structure of the firefighter exam is meticulously designed to evaluate a range of skills and abilities that are crucial for effective firefighting. This comprehensive examination includes several distinct segments, each tailored to assess different facets of a candidate's capabilities. Understanding these segments and the types of questions they encompass is vital for any aspirant, as it sets clear expectations and helps in targeted preparation.

One of the primary segments of the firefighter exam is the written test. This portion typically assesses the candidate's cognitive abilities and theoretical knowledge related to firefighting. Questions in this segment cover a variety of topics, including fire science, building construction, fire control techniques, hazardous materials, and emergency medical care. The questions are designed not only to test knowledge but also to evaluate comprehension and the ability to apply theoretical principles in practical scenarios. Formats may include multiple-choice questions, true/false statements, and scenario-based questions that require critical thinking and quick decision-making.

Another critical component is the physical ability test, which is designed to assess the physical strength, endurance, agility, and overall fitness of the candidates. This segment may include tasks such as climbing stairs or ladders with equipment, dragging hoses, lifting and carrying heavy loads, and performing simulated rescues. These activities mirror the physical demands of actual firefighting work, ensuring that candidates are capable of performing under physically strenuous conditions. The physical tests are not only about strength but also about stamina and efficiency in using one's physical capabilities under pressure.

Additionally, the exam often includes a practical skills test. This part of the examination allows candidates to demonstrate their ability to execute firefighting techniques and emergency response actions. Candidates may be asked to operate firefighting equipment, execute search and rescue operations in smoke-filled environments, or provide basic emergency medical services. This segment tests the hands-on skills and the ability to react effectively in dynamic and potentially hazardous situations.

Some firefighter exams also incorporate a psychological assessment or a personality test. This section aims to evaluate the psychological suitability of the candidates for the high-stress and emotionally taxing nature of firefighting. It may include assessments of traits such as resilience, teamwork capabilities, leadership potential, and the ability to handle stress and make critical decisions during emergencies. These psychological profiles help ensure that candidates are not only physically and intellectually prepared but also emotionally equipped to handle the challenges of the job.

A situational judgment test is another common segment of the firefighter exam. This test assesses the candidate's judgment and decision-making skills in emergency situations. Candidates are presented with hypothetical scenarios related to firefighting and emergency situations and are asked to choose the best course of action among several options. This test measures the candidate's ability to prioritize, make decisions under pressure, and apply logical reasoning in complex situations, which are vital skills on the fireground.

The expectations set for candidates taking the firefighter exam are high, reflecting the demanding nature of the job. Candidates are expected to show a robust blend of knowledge, physical fitness, practical skills, and psychological stability. They are also expected to demonstrate a strong ethical foundation, as firefighters are held to high moral standards, given their role in serving and protecting the community.

Preparation for this exam, therefore, requires a holistic approach. Candidates must engage in physical training to meet the demanding physical requirements, study extensively to cover the breadth of knowledge tested in the written and practical segments and develop the mental resilience and emotional stability required to handle the pressures of emergency response work.

State-by-State Variations: Adapting to Regional Requirements

When preparing for the firefighter exam, it's crucial to understand that not all exams are created equal across the United States. Each state can have its own specific requirements, content, and standards that reflect local laws, firefighting techniques, and emergency response needs. This variability means that candidates need to be well-informed about the particular demands and expectations of the state in which they wish to serve. Adapting to these regional differences is essential for anyone aiming to not only pass the firefighter exam but also to excel as a firefighter within a specific community.

The foundation of these state-by-state variations often lies in the differing nature of fire hazards prevalent in different regions. For example, a state with vast forested areas might emphasize wildland firefighting techniques, while a state with large urban centers might focus more on high-rise fire tactics and rescue operations. These geographical and urban differences directly impact the content and focus of the firefighter exams administered in these regions.

Moreover, the legal framework governing firefighting activities can vary significantly from one state to another. Local building codes, fire safety regulations, and emergency response protocols can differ based on state legislatures and local ordinances. Consequently, the exam in each state may include sections specifically designed to test knowledge of these local laws and regulations. This ensures that firefighters are well-prepared and knowledgeable about the specific conditions and legal requirements of the area they will serve.

In terms of preparation, candidates must first and foremost research and understand the specific requirements of the firefighter exam in the state where they intend to apply. This information is typically available through state fire academies, firefighting agencies, or official state websites. Gaining a clear understanding of the exam structure, the subjects covered, and the practical skills assessed is the first step in tailoring one's study and preparation efforts effectively.

Once the specifics of the state exam are understood, candidates should adjust their study materials and preparation strategies accordingly. For instance, if the state exam places a heavy emphasis on wildland firefighting, candidates should focus on studying fire behavior, safety measures, and containment strategies specific to forest fires. If urban firefighting is more relevant, then understanding the dynamics of fire in high-rise buildings, the use of firefighting equipment in urban settings, and urban search and rescue operations becomes paramount.

Practice tests and preparatory courses that are specifically geared toward the state's exam can be incredibly beneficial. Many educational institutions and online platforms offer resources that are customized for particular state exams. These resources often include practice questions, simulation exercises, and sometimes even tips and strategies from experienced firefighters who have successfully passed the exam in that state.

Furthermore, networking with current firefighters and joining forums or study groups that focus on the state's firefighting exams can provide insights and tips that are not readily available in official study guides. Such interactions can also help candidates understand the practical aspects of firefighting in a specific region, offering a more holistic view of what to expect both during the exam and in their future careers.

Physical preparation should also be tailored according to the specific demands of the state's physical ability test. For instance, if the physical test in a particular state includes a swimming component due to a high number of water-related incidents in the area, candidates will need to ensure that they are proficient swimmers and possibly get specific training in water rescue.

Lastly, understanding the cultural and community aspects of firefighting in a specific state can also play a crucial role in a candidate's preparation and future career. Firefighters are often deeply integrated into the communities they serve, and having knowledge of the local culture, language, and societal norms can enhance a firefighter's effectiveness and integration into the team.

20

CHAPTER 1

CONQUERING READING COMPREHENSION

The importance of reading comprehension in firefighting

Reading comprehension is often underestimated in its importance to firefighting, a profession many associate primarily with physical strength and bravery. However, the ability to effectively understand and process written information is crucial for firefighters, impacting everything from emergency response effectiveness to ongoing education and adherence to safety protocols. This skill is not merely an academic requirement but a critical operational necessity in the high-stakes realm of firefighting.

At the core of firefighting operations is the ability to quickly assimilate and act on complex instructions and information. Firefighting professionals often face situations where they must read and understand detailed reports, instructions, and safety warnings—sometimes under extreme time constraints and stressful conditions. The capacity to read comprehensively ensures that firefighters can interpret these documents accurately, grasp essential details, and execute their tasks effectively.

Moreover, firefighters are required to stay updated with the latest firefighting techniques, equipment manuals, and procedural texts to enhance their skills and knowledge. The field of firefighting is continuously evolving, driven by advances in technology and changes in regulatory frameworks. Manuals, textbooks, and training materials often contain vital information on handling new equipment or executing updated firefighting techniques. A strong command of reading comprehension enables firefighters to learn and apply new information swiftly and correctly, maintaining their effectiveness and safety in responding to calls.

Another critical aspect where reading comprehension plays a vital role is in understanding legal and regulatory documents. Firefighters must be aware of local, state, and national fire codes and regulations to ensure compliance during inspections and operations. Misinterpretations or misunderstandings resulting from poor reading skills can lead to non-compliance, potentially resulting in legal repercussions or, worse, endangering lives during emergency responses.

During emergency operations, firefighters often work with written incident command systems and operation plans. These documents outline strategies and tactics for handling emergencies and require precise understanding to ensure coordination and safety among multiple responders. Effective reading comprehension allows firefighters to quickly absorb the information contained in these plans, translating it into coordinated, tactical actions that can save property and lives.

Moreover, reading comprehension is crucial for effective communication within firefighting teams. Incident reports, logs, and communication from other agencies often contain complex information that firefighters need to interpret and share with their teammates. The ability to read and comprehend these documents ensures that all team members have accurate, up-to-date information, which is essential for the team's operational harmony and effectiveness.

Furthermore, the ability to comprehend written materials extends to the realm of prevention and community education—a significant part of firefighting services. Firefighters often prepare reports for fire incidents and safety inspections and develop educational materials for the community. These tasks require the ability to not only understand complex information but also to convey it simply and effectively to non-professionals. Good reading comprehension skills ensure that firefighters can craft messages that are clear and understandable to the general public, enhancing community safety and engagement.

Additionally, in the context of training and examinations, firefighters are often required to complete written exams that test their knowledge of firefighting practices and protocols. Strong reading comprehension skills are essential for studying for these exams and for understanding the questions properly during the test. This academic aspect of the profession is crucial for advancement and specialization within fire services, highlighting the importance of reading skills even further.

Overview of the exam segment.

The reading comprehension section of the firefighter exam is designed to assess a candidate's ability to quickly and accurately understand written information, a skill fundamental to the duties of a firefighter. This segment of the exam is critical because the ability to interpret and act upon written instructions can significantly impact a firefighter's effectiveness in emergency situations as well as their day-to-day responsibilities.

Typically, this portion of the exam includes a variety of texts that candidates are expected to read and understand. These can range from technical manuals and procedural guidelines to incident reports and informational passages about firefighting techniques or safety protocols. The texts are selected to mimic the types of reading materials that firefighters encounter in their training and professional activities, ensuring that the exam reflects real-world demands.

The types of questions posed in the reading comprehension section are designed to measure a range of cognitive abilities, from basic understanding and recall of facts to more complex analysis and application of information gathered from the texts. Candidates may be asked to discern a passage's major concept or topic, interpret certain words or phrases in light of their context, or draw conclusions from the data presented.

Some questions will test a candidate's ability to discern details that are crucial for accurately following safety measures or operational procedures. For example, a passage might describe a new firefighting technique, followed by questions that ask the candidate to explain how it differs from traditional methods or to identify scenarios where it would be most effective. This tests not only comprehension of the text but also the ability to apply this knowledge practically, a key skill in firefighting operations where understanding nuances can be life-saving.

Additionally, questions may require candidates to analyze the structure or argument of a text. This could involve identifying the author's purpose, distinguishing between facts and opinions, or evaluating the effectiveness of the text in conveying its message. These higher-order thinking skills are essential for firefighters who must often assess complex situations and make informed decisions based on multiple sources of information.

Inference questions are also common in this exam segment. These require candidates to go beyond the information that is explicitly presented and make logical connections. Such questions might involve predicting potential outcomes based on the information in the text or drawing conclusions about the best course of action in a hypothetical scenario described in the passage.

The reading comprehension section also often includes comparative analysis questions where candidates might be asked to compare and contrast different firefighting methods or equipment described in two texts. This ability to weigh and assess multiple viewpoints or sets of data is crucial in the field, where firefighters must often choose the best approach from several alternatives under pressure.

The texts used in the exam are typically written at a level that assumes candidates have a foundational knowledge of firefighting but are also accessible enough that specialized knowledge is not required to understand them. This ensures that the exam is fair and focuses on measuring comprehension skills rather than prior knowledge.

Preparing for this segment of the exam involves practicing with similar texts and question types to develop a quick, efficient reading strategy and the ability to answer questions accurately under time constraints. Candidates might benefit from timed practice sessions that mimic the exam conditions, allowing them to refine their ability to extract necessary information quickly and respond effectively.

Critical Reading Strategies

Techniques for skimming and scanning

In the fast-paced world of firefighting, being able to quickly extract key information from texts—whether they be procedural manuals, incident reports, or regulatory documents—is crucial. The techniques of skimming and scanning are invaluable for this purpose, enabling firefighters and other professionals to identify the most pertinent information efficiently without the need for a thorough read-through. These techniques not only save time but also enhance the ability to respond swiftly and appropriately in situations where every second counts.

Skimming involves running your eyes over a text quickly to get a general idea of the content. This technique is particularly useful when you need to understand the gist or main themes of a document without getting bogged down by the details. When skimming, you typically look for headings, subheadings, highlighted or bolded terms, and any summaries available within the text. These elements are often designed to catch the eye and provide quick insights into the content and structure of the information presented.

To effectively skim a document, start by reading the title and any subtitles or subheadings. These give you immediate clues about what the text is discussing and how the information is organized. After this initial overview, read the first sentence or two of each paragraph. The opening sentences usually contain the main ideas of the paragraphs, and they can tell you whether the details that follow are likely to contain the information you need.

Also, pay attention to any words that are italicized, bolded, or underlined, as these are often used to emphasize important concepts or terminology.

In addition to these strategies, look for any illustrations, charts, or graphs. These can provide a wealth of information at a glance and often support the main textual content. By integrating the visual data with the textual hints provided by your skimming, you can quickly form a comprehensive overview of the document's contents.

Scanning, on the other hand, is a technique used when you know exactly what information you are looking for. It involves moving your eyes rapidly over the text until you find a specific word, phrase, figure, or fact. Scanning is particularly useful for locating particular pieces of information within a large document without reading everything. This could be anything from a specific statistic in a research report to a particular detail in a set of guidelines.

When you begin to scan, it is important to have a clear idea of what you are looking for—be it a date, a name, a keyword, or a specific topic. Once you have this target in mind, let your eyes move quickly over the text, ignoring irrelevant sections and focusing solely on spotting your specific search term. You might find it helpful to use your finger or a pointer to guide your eyes; this can increase your focus and speed as you scan through the content.

Another useful tip for effective scanning is to anticipate where the information might appear in the text based on its layout. For instance, numerical data might be listed in tables, key concepts could be discussed at the beginning of sections, and conclusions can often be found at the end of documents. Predicting the likely location of the information can drastically reduce the time spent scanning.

Both skimming and scanning are enhanced by a good understanding of the text structure. Familiarizing yourself with the common layouts and formats of the types of documents you frequently encounter can significantly speed up your information retrieval process. For example, knowing that incident reports typically start with the event details followed by the response actions can help you quickly locate the information that is most relevant to your immediate needs.

Moreover, practicing these techniques can greatly improve their effectiveness. Regularly engaging in exercises designed to hone your skimming and scanning skills can make them second nature, thereby increasing your speed and accuracy over time. Practice might include timed sessions where you challenge yourself to find specific information in a document or to identify the main ideas of a text as quickly as possible.

In-depth reading vs. surface reading: When and how to apply each

In the realm of information processing, understanding the difference between in-depth reading and surface reading can greatly enhance one's efficiency and effectiveness, particularly in professions where both rapid assimilation of facts and deep comprehension of complex issues are required. Both reading strategies serve distinct purposes and are best utilized in different scenarios.

In-depth reading is the meticulous, analytical approach to processing text, where the reader engages fully with the material, seeking to understand, critique, and internalize the information presented. This method is often time-consuming and requires significant cognitive effort, but it is indispensable for grasping complex concepts, theories, and dense academic or technical materials. It involves reading slowly, often re-reading sections for better understanding and may include taking notes, looking up unfamiliar terms, and synthesizing information from various sources.

In-depth reading is particularly appropriate when learning new topics that require a strong foundational understanding or when one needs to master material for application in critical situations. For instance, firefighters might engage in in-depth reading when studying detailed and technical training manuals about new firefighting techniques or equipment. Understanding the precise mechanics of a new firefighting apparatus, the exact procedure for chemical fire suppression, or the specifications of different fire-resistant materials requires a level of comprehension that only comes from deep, attentive reading.

Techniques for effective in-depth reading include annotating the text, which involves making notes in the margins or on a separate sheet. This can help highlight key points, questions, and counterarguments. Creating summaries after each chapter or section can also aid in reinforcing what has been read, ensuring that the information is processed thoroughly. Additionally, discussing the material with peers or superiors can provide new insights and aid in solidifying understanding.

On the other hand, surface reading involves scanning the text quickly to grasp the main ideas without delving into the underlying details. This approach is less time-intensive and focuses on extracting basic information rather than seeking a deep understanding. Surface reading is suitable in scenarios where a broad comprehension suffices or when sorting through large amounts of information to determine what requires more detailed attention.

For example, a firefighter reviewing incident reports might employ surface reading to quickly sift through routine information while looking out for anomalies or specific details that require further attention. Similarly, when keeping up with new regulations or guidelines, a surface reading can help identify the main themes or changes without getting bogged down in the specifics, which can be revisited more thoroughly if necessary.

Techniques for effective surface reading include focusing on headings, subheadings, bullet points, and any text formatted to stand out, such as bold or italicized words. These elements often contain the crux of the information and can provide a quick understanding of the text's content. Another technique is to read the introduction and conclusion of sections, which often contain summaries of the content, providing a good overview without needing to engage with the entire text.

Choosing between in-depth and surface reading often depends on the purpose of the reading and the nature of the material. For instance, during the initial stages of research or when encountering a large volume of documents, surface reading can help in quickly identifying which materials are relevant and merit closer examination. Once these key materials are identified, switching to in-depth reading ensures that detailed information is not overlooked and is understood comprehensively.

Furthermore, both reading strategies can be employed sequentially as part of a more comprehensive approach to text analysis. Starting with surface reading to get a general overview and then diving deeper into more complex or important segments with in-depth reading can be a practical approach, especially in fields like firefighting, where both quick decision-making and thorough technical knowledge are required.

Tackling Different Question Types

Direct questions: Finding explicit answers

Tackling different types of questions effectively requires a strategic approach, especially when the questions are direct and seek explicit answers. Direct questions are straightforward; they ask for specific information and expect a clear, concise response. These types of questions are common in many scenarios, including exams, interviews, and real-world tasks such as filling out reports or responding to queries.

When encountering direct questions, the first step is to understand exactly what is being asked. This might seem obvious, but under pressure, it's easy to misread or misinterpret the question. Take a moment to read the question carefully, paying close attention to any keywords that specify what the question is targeting. For example, if a question asks, "What is the standard procedure for administering CPR according to the latest guidelines?" the keywords here are "standard procedure," "administering CPR," and "latest guidelines." Recognizing these keywords helps to focus your answer precisely on what is required, avoiding unnecessary details.

Once you've identified what the question is asking, the next step is to recall the relevant information. This is where your preparation and knowledge come into play. For direct questions, it's important to have a well-organized knowledge base from which you can quickly retrieve information. Techniques such as mnemonic devices, mental mapping, or even associating information with specific experiences can facilitate quicker and more accurate recall.

After identifying the relevant information, construct your answer in a clear and structured manner. Direct questions typically do not require elaborate responses but do require accuracy and specificity. For instance, if asked about the temperature at which to store chemical foam extinguishers, your response should directly address the question with the specific temperature without veering into unnecessary details about different types of extinguishers unless explicitly asked.

It's also beneficial to practice articulating your answers clearly and concisely. In high-pressure situations, such as during an exam or in an emergency where clear communication is crucial, the ability to deliver precise information quickly is invaluable. Practicing under timed conditions can help simulate these pressures and prepare you for performing optimally under stress.

Moreover, when preparing for direct questions, it's a good strategy to anticipate potential questions based on the material you are studying. This not only helps in reinforcing your knowledge but also prepares you for the kind of questions you might encounter. Reviewing past exams, if available, or discussing possible questions with peers can provide insights into what kinds of direct questions are typically asked and how best to structure your answers.

In real-world applications, especially in fields like firefighting or emergency medical services, the ability to answer direct questions quickly and accurately can significantly impact the effectiveness of your response to an emergency. For instance, being asked about the correct dosage of a medication or the specifics of a rescue procedure under time-sensitive conditions tests your ability to recall and communicate exact details without hesitation.

Furthermore, enhancing your ability to handle direct questions can also involve using technology or other resources effectively. For professionals in technical fields, quick access to organized data, whether through digital databases or well-maintained logbooks, can facilitate the swift retrieval of factual information. This is particularly useful in scenarios where the information needed is too detailed or voluminous to rely solely on memory.

Finally, the confidence with which you answer direct questions can also influence how your response is perceived, particularly in settings like interviews or team meetings. Confidence, grounded in solid preparation and practice, can make a significant difference in how authoritative and trustworthy your answers appear.

Inference questions: Deriving implicit meanings

Inference questions, unlike direct questions, require one to go beyond the given information to derive implicit meanings based on context, known facts, and logical deduction. These questions are crafted to evaluate one's ability to think critically and make connections that are not explicitly stated, making them particularly challenging and essential in both academic settings and real-world applications.

When tackling inference questions, the initial approach involves a deep understanding of the text or situation presented. This means not only grasping the literal information but also paying attention to nuances and subtleties that might indicate broader themes or conclusions. In the context of reading comprehension, for instance, it is crucial to consider the tone, word choice, and structure of the text, as these elements can provide significant insights into the author's intentions and the text's underlying messages.

The key to successfully answering inference questions lies in careful observation and critical thinking. You must be able to discern patterns or connections that suggest a conclusion different from what is directly presented. For example, if a passage describes a character's actions quietly packing away their office belongings and looking around nostalgically, an inference question might ask why the character is packing. The answer would not be found explicitly in the text but could be inferred from the described actions and emotional undertone—perhaps the character is leaving the job or retiring.

Effective strategies for handling inference questions include hypothesizing and then using the text to validate your hypotheses. Start by asking yourself what the implicit message or fact could be based on the information provided. Then, scan the text to find evidence that supports or refutes your hypothesis. This method ensures that your inferences are grounded in the text, even though they extend beyond its explicit content.

Another crucial aspect of tackling inference questions is distinguishing between what is directly stated and what is implied. This distinction is critical because it prevents the confusion of assumptions with inferences. Assumptions are beliefs held without proof or explicit evidence, whereas inferences are conclusions reached based on evidence and reasoning. For instance, if a text mentions that someone spends a lot of time in the library, one might infer that the person enjoys reading or studying rather than assuming they work there unless more specific details suggest otherwise.

Practice plays a pivotal role in mastering inference questions. Engaging with diverse texts and scenarios helps develop a keener sense of nuances that typically inform inference. Academic exercises, critical reading materials, and even discussion groups can provide practice in identifying and articulating implicit meanings. Discussions, in particular, can expose you to different perspectives and inference strategies, enriching your ability to think divergently and deeply about possible meanings hidden beneath the surface.

In real-world contexts, especially in professional fields such as law, psychology, and even technical disciplines like engineering, the ability to make accurate inferences can significantly impact decision-making and problem-solving. For example, a doctor might need to infer a diagnosis based on a combination of medical symptoms that do not point explicitly to a particular condition. Similarly, a project manager might infer potential project risks based on subtle signs of team discontent or supplier issues.

Moreover, in interpersonal communications within workplace environments, inference helps in understanding non-verbal cues and implied meanings in conversations, which can be crucial for maintaining good relationships and effective communication. The ability to infer emotional states or intentions without them being explicitly communicated can lead to more sensitive and appropriate interactions.

Vocabulary and context analysis.

Vocabulary and context analysis are critical components in tackling various types of questions, particularly in understanding complex texts and environments. This skill involves more than just knowing the definitions of words; it requires an understanding of how language works within different contexts, how word choices can affect meaning, and how nuances of language can significantly influence interpretation and response.

Effective vocabulary and context analysis start with a robust knowledge base of vocabulary. This doesn't merely entail the ability to recognize or define words but also includes understanding their connotations and denotations, synonyms and antonyms, and their usage in different phrases or idiomatic expressions. Expanding vocabulary is a continual process that benefits immensely from wide reading, active learning, and regular practice. Engaging with diverse materials — from technical articles and literature to everyday communication — helps in encountering words in various contexts, which strengthens understanding and retention.

When analyzing vocabulary within a context, it's crucial to consider the surrounding words and the overall theme of the text. Words can have different meanings based on their usage in a sentence or paragraph. For example, the word "draft" can refer to a preliminary version of a piece of writing, a flow of air, or the compulsory recruitment for military service, depending on the context in which it is used. Being able to discern which meaning is appropriate in a given situation is key to correctly interpreting and responding to questions, especially in exams or critical professional scenarios.

Another aspect of vocabulary and context analysis is understanding how context shapes the meaning of a text or conversation. This includes the cultural, historical, and situational contexts. For instance, certain phrases or terms might be understood differently in one culture compared to another or even within different subgroups of the same culture. Historical context can also provide essential insights, especially in understanding texts that refer to specific events, beliefs, or attitudes prevalent at a particular time.

A practical technique for improving context analysis skills is to practice with varied and challenging texts, intentionally focusing on how words and phrases function differently in diverse contexts. Questions and exercises that ask you to interpret or rephrase sentences, predict outcomes based on given scenarios, or identify the tone or mood of passages are particularly useful. These activities encourage deeper engagement with the text and enhance your ability to derive meaning from subtle linguistic cues.

Additionally, engaging in discussions about texts or scenarios can further enhance your vocabulary and context analysis skills. Explaining your interpretation and hearing others' perspectives can illuminate different ways that language might be understood or applied. Such discussions often highlight the subjective nature of language and reinforce the importance of considering multiple viewpoints.

In real-world applications, strong vocabulary and context analysis skills are invaluable in any profession that relies on effective communication. Whether it's drafting a precise legal document, interpreting medical notes, executing project plans, or resolving customer complaints, the ability to understand and use language appropriately within different contexts can lead to better outcomes and clearer communication. For instance, in customer service, recognizing the emotional tone behind a customer's words can help tailor responses to better address their concerns and de-escalate potential conflicts.

Furthermore, the effectiveness and integrity of one's work may be greatly impacted by one's ability to analyze terminology and context, particularly in disciplines like law, psychology, and journalism, where accuracy and clarity of language are critical. It guarantees that the target audience understands the message correctly and that it serves the desired goal.

Dear Readers,

Thank you for reading the first chapter of our comprehensive guide to preparing for the firefighter exam. We hope the insights and strategies shared here have been helpful and informative. If this chapter has met or exceeded your expectations, we'd be grateful if you could take a few minutes to leave a review on Amazon. Your feedback is invaluable to us, helping to improve future editions of the book and assisting fellow readers in making informed decisions.

How You Can Share Your Review:

Through Amazon.com:

1. Go to the Amazon page where you found my book.

2. Navigate to the 'Customer Reviews' section.

3. Click on 'Write a customer review' to share your valuable insights.

Instant QR Code Access: Simply scan the QR code below with your smartphone to be directed to the Amazon review section.

CHAPTER 2

MASTERING MATHEMATICAL REASONING

The Quantitative Edge

The role of math in firefighting

The role of mathematics in firefighting is both vital and multifaceted, impacting nearly every aspect of the profession, from the basic operations on the ground to the strategic decisions made at higher levels of fire management. Mathematical reasoning provides a framework through which firefighters can understand and predict various dynamics of fire behavior, effectively allocate resources, and ensure safety during operations.

At the most immediate level, firefighters use mathematics to calculate the amount of water required to extinguish a fire. This calculation involves several variables, including the type and amount of fuel burning, the heat output of the fire, and the efficiency of the water delivery system. Understanding the relationship between these variables allows firefighters to use their resources more effectively, ensuring that they can deliver a sufficient volume of water to the fire to cool the flames and prevent their spread.

Moreover, the principles of hydraulics are central to firefighting, as water must often be transported over long distances through hoses and pumps. Firefighters use mathematical formulas to calculate pressure loss in fire hoses, which depends on hose diameter, length, and the velocity of the water.

By accurately calculating these factors, firefighters can ensure that water maintains sufficient pressure to reach and suppress the fire effectively. This is crucial in large-scale or high-rise fires where water must be pumped over extended distances or heights.

Another critical area where mathematical reasoning is employed is in the calculation of fire load and fire resistance. Fire load refers to the maximum amount of heat that can be produced if all combustible materials in a given area burn. Knowing the fire load helps in assessing the potential severity of a fire, which in turn informs the tactics that firefighters use in combating the blaze. Similarly, understanding the fire resistance of different building materials — which involves calculations based on material properties, thickness, and density — helps firefighters predict how long structural elements of a building will withstand before collapsing. For the safety of the firemen and any people who may still be inside the structure, this information is essential.

Mathematics also plays a role in the strategic placement of fire stations and the deployment of fire suppression resources. Using algorithms and statistical models, fire departments analyze historical data on fire incidents to identify patterns and predict future fire risks. This analysis helps in optimizing the locations of fire stations to ensure quick response times across various regions. Furthermore, resource allocation models help determine the number and type of firefighting resources — such as trucks, hoses, and personnel — required to effectively respond to fires within a specific area.

In the realm of hazardous materials (hazmat) incidents, mathematical models are used to predict the behavior of toxic chemicals in the event of a spill or leak. These models take into account factors such as the amount of material, its physical and chemical properties, and environmental conditions like wind speed and direction. The results help firefighters decide on evacuation areas, containment strategies, and cleanup procedures, significantly mitigating the potential harm to the public and the environment.

Moreover, the growing use of technology in firefighting, such as Geographic Information Systems (GIS) and drones, relies heavily on mathematics. GIS uses spatial data and mathematical models to map fire incidents and simulate fire spread scenarios, providing valuable insights that guide decision-making during fire suppression efforts. Drones equipped with thermal imaging cameras offer real-time data that is analyzed mathematically to assess hot spots and the effectiveness of firefighting efforts, allowing commanders to make informed tactical decisions.

Firefighting also involves a significant amount of training and simulation, much of which is underpinned by mathematical concepts. Simulations of fire scenarios use complex mathematical models to mimic fire behaviors under different conditions. These simulations help in training firefighters, allowing them to experience and react to a variety of fire scenarios in a controlled, virtual environment.

Overview of the mathematical reasoning section

The Mathematical Reasoning section of the firefighter exam is designed to assess a candidate's ability to apply mathematical concepts and techniques to solve practical problems, a fundamental skill required in firefighting operations. This section tests a range of mathematical skills, from basic arithmetic to more complex algebra and geometry, reflecting the diverse mathematical challenges a firefighter might encounter in the field.

The structure of the Mathematical Reasoning section typically includes a series of problems that require candidates to perform calculations, interpret data, and apply mathematical principles to real-world scenarios. These problems are often presented in multiple-choice format, which requires candidates not only to perform calculations accurately but also to choose the correct answer from several possibilities, ensuring that they understand the problem and the steps needed to solve it.

Types of problems in this section can vary widely but generally include the following categories:

1. **Basic Arithmetic and Algebra**: These problems test the candidate's ability to perform basic computations such as addition, subtraction, multiplication, and division. They also include questions on fractions, decimals, ratios, proportions, and percentages. Algebra problems might involve solving equations or inequalities, working with algebraic expressions, and understanding relationships between variables. These skills are essential for tasks such as calculating flow rates, determining the correct mix of chemicals in fire suppression, or estimating areas and perimeters when dealing with fire safety plans.

2. **Geometry**: This includes questions on the properties of shapes, calculating areas and volumes of various geometric figures, and understanding the Pythagorean theorem. Geometry is crucial in firefighting for tasks such as calculating the amount of material needed to cover a specific area, determining the reach of ladders, or assessing the structural stability of buildings based on their geometric design.

3. **Word Problems**: These problems require candidates to extract relevant information from textual descriptions and then use mathematics to solve the problems. Word problems are particularly important as they simulate real-life situations a firefighter might face, such as calculating the time required to fill or drain a tank, determining the force needed to break through obstacles, or estimating how long a supply of resources will last during an operation.

4. **Data Interpretation**: This category includes questions that involve interpreting graphs, tables, and charts. Firefighters must often analyze data from various sources to make informed decisions quickly. For example, understanding trends in data can help predict fire behavior or evaluate the effectiveness of firefighting strategies over time.

5. **Applied Mathematics**: These problems are specifically tailored to reflect the practical application of mathematics in firefighting. They

might involve scenarios such as calculating the expansion of fire in different conditions, determining the optimal path or angles for hose deployment, or applying principles of hydraulics and mechanics to firefighting equipment operations.

The Mathematical Reasoning section is timed, adding an element of pressure that tests a candidate's ability to use these skills efficiently under exam conditions, mirroring the time-sensitive nature of real firefighting situations. Candidates are typically allowed to use a basic calculator, ensuring that the focus is on problem-solving and application rather than simple computation.

Preparation for this section of the exam usually involves reviewing mathematical concepts, practicing with sample problems, and taking timed practice tests to improve speed and accuracy. Understanding the types of questions and the format of the section helps candidates develop effective strategies for tackling this part of the exam, enhancing their overall performance.

Essential Mathematical Concepts

Basic arithmetic and algebra

Basic arithmetic and algebra form the bedrock of the mathematical reasoning required in many professional fields, including firefighting. These fundamental skills are essential for understanding and solving the diverse quantitative challenges encountered during firefighting operations.

Basic Arithmetic

In firefighting, basic arithmetic is used daily. Firefighters often need to calculate distances, areas, volumes, and other measurements related to fire scenes and safety plans. For example, calculating the amount of water required to extinguish a fire involves basic arithmetic to ensure the correct volume of water is pumped at the right rate. Firefighters might also need to determine how long it will take to reach a location at a given speed or how much foam to use in conjunction with water to effectively fight chemical fires.

Basic arithmetic operations—addition, subtraction, multiplication, and division—are employed to manage resources effectively. This might include dividing teams into groups, distributing equipment among crew members, or calculating the time shifts needed for full coverage without exhausting any single team. In emergency medical situations, firefighters use arithmetic to calculate dosages for medications or to mix solutions for patients.

Moreover, when managing fire incidents, firefighters are often tasked with estimating the potential expansion of fire, requiring them to quickly compute areas affected by the fire to coordinate effective containment strategies. Accurate calculations ensure that response efforts are proportionate and effective, preventing the waste of valuable resources.

Algebra

While basic arithmetic deals with numbers directly, algebra introduces the use of variables and formulas, which are crucial in making predictions and solving problems where some information is unknown. In firefighting, algebraic reasoning is used to solve for unknowns in various operational scenarios.

One common application is the use of formulas to determine the pressure needed in fire hoses to achieve a specific water flow rate at a fire's location. The formula might include variables representing hose diameter, water velocity, and hose length—factors that determine the pressure drop as water moves through the hose. By rearranging these formulas, firefighters can solve for the unknown variable, such as the maximum length of hose that can be used without losing the necessary pressure to suppress the fire.

Algebra is also used in the strategic planning of resources. For instance, firefighters use algebra to create models that predict the spread of fire based on various factors such as wind speed, the type of materials burning, and the area's topography. These models often involve equations that help firefighters decide how to allocate resources most effectively to mitigate the fire's impact.

Furthermore, understanding and applying algebraic equations is crucial when dealing with hazardous materials. Firefighters may use algebra to calculate the safe distance for evacuation around a gas leak, considering factors such as the amount and type of gas, the leak's rate, and environmental conditions. These calculations are vital for ensuring public safety and effective incident management.

To prepare for scenarios requiring basic arithmetic and algebra, firefighters often engage in training and exercises that simulate real-life situations. This training helps them refine their mathematical skills and apply them under pressure, ensuring they are ready to perform these calculations quickly and accurately during actual fire incidents.

Geometry and statistics basics for firefighters

Geometry and statistics are critical mathematical disciplines that play significant roles in firefighting operations, helping to ensure effective decision-making, resource allocation, and strategic planning.

Geometry in Firefighting

Geometry is used extensively in firefighting to solve problems related to space, shapes, and volumes, which are crucial for various operational tasks. For instance, firefighters use geometry to calculate the area affected by a fire, which is essential for determining the amount of suppressant needed, whether water, foam, or another agent. This calculation helps in preparing adequate resources without wasting materials, ensuring an efficient response to fire emergencies.

The principles of geometry also come into play when determining the reach of ladders or the positioning of fire trucks. Firefighters might calculate the angle and proper placement of ladders to safely reach specific heights or distances. This involves understanding the properties of triangles and the

Pythagorean theorem to ensure that ladders are placed at safe and effective angles for climbing.

Moreover, the layout of buildings and the arrangement of rooms often require firefighters to have a good grasp of spatial geometry. This knowledge allows them to navigate complex structures more effectively, especially when visibility is low due to smoke or darkness. Understanding floor plans and being able to mentally map out spaces can be lifesaving in rescue operations.

In the case of hazardous materials incidents, geometry helps in creating exclusion zones, which are areas cordoned off to prevent access due to potential hazards. Calculating the radius of these zones involves understanding circle geometry and the principles of diffusion and dispersion, which dictate how materials spread from a single point.

Statistics in Firefighting

Statistics play a pivotal role in firefighting, primarily in risk assessment, resource management, and strategic planning. Fire departments routinely collect and analyze data on fire incidents, response times, outcomes, and resource usage. This statistical analysis helps in identifying trends and patterns that inform the development of more effective firefighting strategies and public safety policies.

For example, by analyzing the frequency and locations of fires within a community, fire departments can optimize the placement of fire stations to ensure the quickest possible response times across different areas. Statistical models can also predict the likelihood of fire incidents in various districts based on factors such as building age, type, and previous fire history, allowing for more proactive fire prevention efforts.

Statistics are also used in the evaluation of firefighting techniques and equipment. Through the analysis of performance data, fire departments can assess the effectiveness of different firefighting methods or tools under various conditions. This helps in making evidence-based decisions about investments in new technologies or techniques.

Moreover, statistical methods help in the management of personnel and scheduling. Analyzing data related to shifts, incident reports, and personnel performance allows for efficient scheduling that maximizes coverage while minimizing fatigue among firefighters.

Firefighting also utilizes statistics in the realm of public education and community outreach. By understanding the statistics related to common causes of fires and the demographics most affected by fire incidents, fire departments can tailor their education programs to target specific risks and populations. This targeted approach helps in significantly reducing fire risks and improving community safety.

Problem-Solving Techniques

Step-by-step approaches to solving typical exam problems

Problem-solving is a critical skill for firefighters, both in the field and when tackling the mathematical reasoning section of firefighter exams. Effective problem-solving often involves a systematic approach that allows for clear thinking, even under pressure, which is crucial during emergencies or in the high-stress environment of an exam.

A well-structured approach to solving problems typically begins with carefully reading and understanding the question. This step is vital because misinterpreting the question can lead to incorrect answers, no matter how well the subsequent calculations are executed. Candidates are encouraged to read the question several times and to underline or highlight key information that will influence their approach to solving the problem. This could include noting whether the problem is asking for a specific calculation, a theoretical explanation, or the application of a concept to a practical scenario.

Once the problem is clearly understood, the next step is to plan the approach. This involves identifying which mathematical principles or formulas are applicable. For instance, if the problem involves calculating water flow rates for firefighting, knowing the appropriate hydraulic formulas and understanding how variables like hose diameter and water pressure affect the flow rate is crucial. At this stage, sketching diagrams or listing known variables and what needs to be determined can help clarify thoughts and guide the problem-solving process.

The execution of the plan is the next step. This involves applying the chosen mathematical methods or formulas to the information provided in the problem. It's important to work systematically, ensuring that each step of the calculation is followed accurately and logically. During this phase, maintaining neatness and organization in the work can prevent confusion, especially with complex calculations that involve multiple steps or variables.

It is also advisable to check the calculations at this stage. Simple errors such as misplaced decimal points or incorrect unit conversions can drastically alter the outcome. Double-checking not only the final answer but also intermediate steps can catch these mistakes early. Using a calculator for arithmetic calculations can help improve accuracy, but relying on mental checks for conceptual understanding is equally important.

After calculating an answer, it is essential to review the result in the context of the problem. This involves considering whether the answer makes sense given the scenario. For example, if calculating the amount of water needed to suppress a fire, does the answer seem reasonable based on the size of the fire and the conditions described? Asking these types of questions can reveal errors in reasoning or calculation that might have been overlooked.

Finally, it's beneficial to reflect on the problem-solving process itself once the problem is completed. This reflection isn't just about whether the right answer was found but also about how efficient and effective the chosen method was. Could there have been a simpler, more direct way to solve the problem? What lessons can be learned for similar problems in the future? This reflective practice enhances a candidate's problem-solving skills over time, making them more adept at tackling various types of questions with confidence.

In practical firefighting scenarios, this problem-solving approach is equally valuable. Whether it's calculating the optimal way to ventilate a smoke-filled structure or determining the best angle to position a ladder for a rescue, the ability to systematically assess and address challenges can make the difference between success and failure in emergency operations. Thus, honing these problem-solving techniques in an exam setting is not just about passing a test; it's about preparing for real-world firefighting tasks where lives and properties may depend on a firefighter's quick thinking and mathematical acuity.

Common mathematical traps and how to avoid them.

In tackling mathematical problems, especially under the time constraints of an exam or in high-pressure scenarios like firefighting, it's easy to fall into common traps. These traps can lead to incorrect answers and misguided decisions despite a good understanding of the underlying mathematical concepts. Being aware of these pitfalls and knowing how to avoid them can significantly enhance the accuracy and reliability of one's calculations.

One common mathematical trap is misreading the problem. This might sound simple, yet in the rush to answer questions, especially during exams, it's easy to skim too quickly and miss crucial details. For instance, a problem might ask for the diameter of a hose but is answered with the radius, or it might require an answer in square meters, but it's mistakenly given in square feet. To avoid this trap, take the time to read each problem carefully, underline or highlight key terms, and double-check what the question is actually asking. This careful reading ensures that you're solving for the correct variable and using the appropriate units.

Another frequent issue is unit conversion errors. Firefighting problems often involve units like gallons and liters or feet and meters, and converting between these can lead to mistakes if not done carefully. Always double-check conversion factors and ensure you're converting units consistently throughout your calculations. Keeping a small cheat sheet of common conversion factors handy during an exam, if allowed, can be very helpful.

Over-reliance on calculators is another trap. While calculators are incredibly useful tools, relying on them without understanding the underlying mathematics can lead to errors, especially if a wrong key is pressed accidentally. To combat this, it's advisable to estimate answers mentally first. This rough estimation not only provides a sanity check against the calculator's output but also deepens your understanding of the problem by forcing you to engage more deeply with the mathematical concepts involved.

Misapplying formulas is also a common trap. In the heat of the moment, it's easy to apply a familiar formula without considering whether it's appropriate for the current scenario. To prevent this, familiarize yourself not just with the formulas but with the conditions under which they apply. When practicing, take time after solving each problem to reflect on why a particular formula was used and what could happen if it was misapplied. This reflection builds a deeper understanding that can prevent misapplication under exam conditions or in real-world applications.

Skipping steps in a hurry to get to the answer can lead to mistakes, particularly in multi-step problems common in firefighting scenarios, such as calculating pressures in hydraulic systems or determining the load capacity of the equipment. Always work through problems methodically, writing down each step. This practice not only minimizes errors but also makes it easier to review your work and catch mistakes if the final answer doesn't seem right.

Finally, confirmation bias is a subtle yet significant trap. This occurs when solving problems under preconceived notions about what the answer should be, leading to disregarding actual calculations that point to a different conclusion. To avoid this, approach each problem with an open mind, rely on the data and calculations rather than assumptions, and be ready to accept unexpected results if the mathematics supports them.

Being aware of these common traps and adopting strategies to avoid them enhances not only performance on mathematical exams but also the effectiveness and safety of firefighting operations. By fostering a careful, methodical approach to problem-solving, firefighters can ensure that their mathematical calculations are as reliable and accurate as possible, supporting their critical and lifesaving missions.

CHAPTER 3

MECHANICAL REASONING UNLOCKED

Mechanics in Firefighting

The importance of mechanical reasoning.

Mechanical reasoning is a crucial skill for firefighters, underpinning many aspects of their daily responsibilities and emergency responses. This skill involves understanding and applying mechanical concepts and principles, which are integral to operating equipment, solving problems, and making decisions during firefighting operations.

The nature of firefighting requires the use of various mechanical tools and devices, from simple levers and pulleys to more complex machinery like pumps and hydraulic systems. A solid grasp of mechanical reasoning enables firefighters to operate this equipment efficiently and safely. For instance, understanding how a pump generates pressure and how this affects water flow through hoses is critical when battling fires. Firefighters must be able to adjust pressures and flows based on the specific needs of the situation, such as changing the spray pattern to combat different types of fires or adjusting the flow rate to conserve water while ensuring effective firefighting.

Moreover, mechanical reasoning is essential for troubleshooting and maintaining equipment. Firefighting gear must function correctly at all times since equipment failures can have dire consequences during emergencies. Firefighters with acute mechanical reasoning skills can often identify and correct issues with their equipment, ensuring that everything is in optimal working condition. This not only helps in maintaining the equipment but also in preventing potential malfunctions that could impede firefighting efforts or compromise safety.

In addition, mechanical reasoning aids in understanding the dynamics of fire and building structures. Firefighters often deal with complex situations where they need to assess the integrity of burning buildings or decide the best method for forced entry. Knowledge of mechanical principles such as force, torque, and the properties of materials helps firefighters make informed decisions about which areas of a building are likely to be structurally compromised or how to apply force effectively to breach doors or windows without causing unintended damage.

Rescue operations are another area where mechanical reasoning is indispensable. Many rescue scenarios involve the use of ropes, winches, and pulleys, particularly in high-angle or confined space rescues. Firefighters must understand the principles behind these systems, such as how pulleys distribute weight and how to set up systems that can safely bear loads. This knowledge ensures that they can rig rescue equipment safely and efficiently, enhancing their ability to save lives under difficult conditions.

Furthermore, mechanical reasoning is critical in hazardous materials incidents, where understanding the mechanics of containers and the behavior of various substances under pressure can prevent accidents. When dealing with hazardous materials, firefighters must make calculations and decisions about how to contain substances, mitigate leaks, and prevent explosions. Proficiency in mechanical reasoning allows for a better understanding of how changes in temperature and pressure can affect chemical stability and container integrity, guiding effective response strategies.

Training in mechanical reasoning typically involves both theoretical and practical components, ensuring that firefighters are not only familiar with mechanical concepts but also adept at applying them in real-world situations. This combination of knowledge and application is cultivated through continuous education and practice, both at the fire academy and on the job.

Overview of the Mechanical Reasoning section

The Mechanical Reasoning section of the firefighter exam is a critical component designed to test a candidate's ability to understand and apply mechanical principles in practical situations. This section evaluates the understanding of basic physical laws and mechanical operations, which are fundamental to daily firefighting tasks, ranging from operating equipment to handling emergency scenarios where quick mechanical thinking is necessary.

Candidates facing the Mechanical Reasoning section can expect a variety of questions that simulate the kinds of mechanical challenges they will encounter in their roles as firefighters. This segment of the exam typically includes visual diagrams, practical problem scenarios, and multiple-choice questions that require the application of mechanical concepts such as levers, pulleys, gears, inclines, and screws. Each question aims to assess the candidate's ability to analyze, interpret, and solve mechanical problems using these principles.

For instance, a typical question might present a diagram of a pulley system used to lift equipment and ask the candidate to determine the force required to raise the load to a certain height. This type of question tests knowledge of the basic principles of physics that govern the operation of pulleys, including the understanding of force distribution and load management. Other questions may involve gears and ask candidates to predict the direction and speed of rotating gear systems when a certain gear is turned in a specified way. Understanding how gears interact is crucial not only in tackling such exam questions but also in real-life firefighting scenarios where equipment with gear mechanisms might be used.

Furthermore, candidates may encounter questions involving hydraulic systems, which are common in the operation of firefighting equipment. These questions might ask for calculations related to fluid pressure and flow rate in hoses or pumps, requiring an understanding of hydraulics principles. The ability to quickly calculate these factors can significantly affect firefighting effectiveness, particularly when dealing with fires that require large volumes of water delivered at specific pressures.

The Mechanical Reasoning section also often includes scenarios that require a combination of mechanical knowledge and practical problem-solving skills. For example, a question might describe a situation where a firefighter needs to stabilize a vehicle at an accident scene using jacks or chocks and ask the candidate to choose the best placement and type of equipment to use based on the vehicle's weight and position. This tests not only the candidate's understanding of stability and leverage but also their ability to apply these concepts under pressure to ensure safety and efficiency.

In preparing for this section, candidates are advised to thoroughly study the principles of mechanics and physics as they apply to firefighting. Practical experience with mechanical tools and systems, such as those found in automotive or industrial settings, can be incredibly beneficial. Additionally, engaging in study groups or courses that focus on mechanical reasoning and offer practice questions and tests can help candidates develop a stronger grasp of necessary concepts and improve their test-taking strategies.

During the exam, it is important for candidates to carefully read each question and analyze all diagrams and additional information provided. A methodical approach is crucial—taking the time to understand each problem fully before attempting a solution ensures that errors are minimized. Double-checking calculations and considering different angles of a problem can help uncover insights that might initially be overlooked.

Candidates should also manage their time efficiently during this section of the exam. While it is important to solve each problem accurately, spending too much time on one question can jeopardize the ability to complete the section. Practicing timed quizzes and learning shortcuts for common calculations can enhance time management skills, ensuring that candidates can demonstrate their mechanical reasoning abilities effectively within the exam's constraints.

Ultimately, the Mechanical Reasoning section is not just about testing knowledge of mechanical concepts; it's about assessing a candidate's ability to apply this knowledge in practical, often high-stakes situations. Success in this exam section indicates readiness to handle the mechanical aspects of firefighting, where quick thinking, problem-solving, and a solid understanding of mechanical principles are key to performing safely and effectively in the field.

Principles of Mechanics

Levers, pulleys, gears, and inclined planes

Understanding the principles of mechanics is crucial in many technical and engineering fields, including firefighting, where knowledge of levers, pulleys, gears, and inclined planes can significantly impact the effectiveness and safety of operations. These mechanical principles are not just theoretical concepts; they are practical tools that firefighters use daily to enhance their efficiency and ensure their safety in various emergency situations.

Simple devices called levers are made of a rigid rod or beam that is pivoting at a fixed hinge or fulcrum. In firefighting, levers are commonly used in tools like pry bars or Halligan bars, which are employed to open doors or move heavy debris. The principle of the lever allows firefighters to apply a smaller force over a greater distance at one end of the lever to achieve a greater force over a shorter distance at the other end, effectively multiplying their force to accomplish tasks that would otherwise require much greater physical effort. This principle is vital when creating openings or displacing obstacles in rescue operations quickly.

Pulleys are another simple machine that is used to lift heavy loads with less effort. A pulley system can be set up using a wheel on an axle and a rope or cable, which can change the direction of the applied force and, depending on the configuration, also multiply the force. This is especially useful in firefighting for hoisting equipment or lowering rescuers into confined spaces. The use of compound pulleys, where multiple wheels are combined, allows for distributing the load more evenly and reducing the amount of force needed from each firefighter, making it a critical component in managing energy and reducing fatigue during prolonged operations.

Gears, which are wheels with teeth that interlock to transmit torque, are fundamental in the machinery used in firefighting, such as in the mechanisms of fire engines, ladders, and pumps. Gears ensure that these pieces of equipment operate smoothly and efficiently, translating rotational motion into the necessary action with precision and reliability. Understanding how gears interact and affect each other is crucial for maintaining and troubleshooting firefighting apparatus. For example, if a pump's gears malfunction, knowing the principles of how gears operate can help quickly identify the problem and possibly fix it, ensuring minimal downtime during critical moments.

Inclined planes, or ramps, are used to move heavy loads vertically with less force. The slope of the inclined plane allows for spreading the effort needed to elevate a load over a longer distance, decreasing the force required at any given moment. This principle is utilized in firefighting when elevating equipment or even casualties on stretchers from lower to higher ground or through uneven terrain. Inclined planes reduce the physical strain on firefighters, enabling them to conserve energy for other demanding tasks at the scene.

Each of these mechanical principles has direct implications for firefighting tactics and safety. Knowing how to leverage these principles allows firefighters to perform their duties more effectively, conserving energy, reducing risk, and potentially saving more lives. For instance, during an auto extrication, understanding the mechanical advantage provided by a lever can determine the quickest way to free a trapped person without causing further injury.

Furthermore, the ability to apply these principles in real time can significantly enhance problem-solving capabilities in dynamic and unpredictable environments. Firefighting often involves rapidly changing conditions where the initial response strategy may need to be adjusted. A deep understanding of mechanics can facilitate swift and informed adjustments that optimize the response to evolving situations.

Moreover, training in mechanical reasoning is not only about personal performance but also about team efficiency. Firefighting is intensely collaborative, and operations often involve coordinating multiple team members and pieces of equipment to tackle complex scenarios effectively. A team that collectively understands and can apply mechanical principles will be better equipped to strategize, distribute tasks, and deploy resources in the most effective manner.

In addition to enhancing operational capabilities, knowledge of mechanical principles is also critical for safety. When mechanical tools and principles are used properly, forces and loads may be regulated safely, preventing workplace accidents and injuries. It is also essential to keep the firefighting apparatus in excellent working order to function dependably in emergency scenarios.

Understanding force and torque

Understanding force and torque is essential across many scientific and engineering disciplines, particularly in fields requiring the manipulation of physical systems, such as mechanical engineering and physics, and also in more practical fields like firefighting. Force and torque are foundational concepts that describe how objects interact and influence each other mechanically, and mastering these concepts can greatly enhance the effectiveness and safety of operations in such practical fields.

Force is a push or a pull upon an object resulting from its interaction with another object. It has both magnitude and direction, making it a vector quantity. When a force is applied to an object, it can cause the object to accelerate, slow down, remain in place, or change shape. The application of force is observed daily in tasks such as lifting, pushing, pulling, and even in the act of standing still, where the force of gravity interacts with the body.

Torque, on the other hand, is a measure of the force that can cause an object to rotate about an axis. Like force, torque also has magnitude and direction. Torque is the rotational equivalent of linear force and is calculated as the product of the force and the distance from the point of rotation, or pivot point, to where the force is applied. This distance is referred to as the moment arm. Torque is particularly evident in any scenario involving turning objects, from opening a bottle cap to adjusting a fire hose nozzle or using a wrench.

In firefighting, understanding these principles is crucial when using tools and equipment that require precise control to manage fires effectively and safely. For instance, when using a pry bar to open a jammed door or lift heavy debris, firefighters need to apply the right amount of force at the correct angle to maximize the bar's leverage while minimizing their own effort and exposure to risk.

Moreover, the concept of torque plays a significant role when firefighters need to handle equipment such as ladders or when operating valves on fire hydrants and water pumps. A clear understanding of how torque works allows firefighters to apply force effectively to open or close valves, which may be highly resistant due to pressure, rust, or damage. Calculating the necessary torque to apply for turning these valves can prevent damage to the equipment and avoid physical strain or injury.

Force and torque also underpin the mechanics of water movement within hoses. Firefighting hoses deal with high-pressure water, and managing these hoses requires a good grasp of how forces act on different parts of the hose system, including the nozzles and couplings. Balancing the forces caused by high-pressure water helps in controlling the hose effectively, preventing it from whipping violently or causing injury. Firefighters calculate the required hose diameters, water velocity, and pressure to manage the force output effectively, ensuring sufficient reach and impact of the water stream on the fire.

The principles of force and torque also extend to the design and use of firefighting vehicles and machinery. Fire engines are equipped with various mechanical systems, such as pumps and aerial ladders, that rely on hydraulic systems, which operate based on principles of force and torque. Understanding these principles allows firefighters to operate such machinery safely and efficiently, ensuring they can reach higher floors of buildings to rescue individuals or to better target water streams.

Furthermore, in rescue operations involving car accidents, firefighters often use hydraulic rescue tools—commonly known as the 'Jaws of Life'—to cut through vehicle structures to free trapped individuals. The operation of these tools involves the precise application of force and understanding the torque required to cut through metal without causing additional harm or destabilizing the vehicle further.

In training, firefighters engage extensively with scenarios that test and refine their understanding of these mechanical principles. Training drills often simulate real-life situations where quick calculation and application of force and torque are necessary, reinforcing the practical importance of these concepts.

Mechanical Aptitude in Action

Real-world applications in firefighting equipment and scenarios

Mechanical aptitude plays a crucial role in firefighting, a field where knowledge and application of mechanical principles can have immediate life-saving impacts. Understanding the mechanics behind equipment and scenarios enables firefighters to operate more effectively and safely in the demanding and often hazardous environments they face. This aptitude encompasses a wide range of applications, from the operation of complex machinery to the execution of rescue operations, all of which rely on a deep understanding of how things work.

One of the most direct applications of mechanical aptitude in firefighting is the use of various types of pumps and engines, which are central to nearly all firefighting efforts. Fire engines are equipped with pumps that must deliver water at high pressures to hoses, a process that requires precise understanding and manipulation of mechanical components to ensure the right amount of force and flow. Firefighters must understand the relationship between engine speed, pump pressure, and hose diameter to optimize the delivery of water to suppress fires effectively. This knowledge ensures that the water pressure is neither too low, which would be ineffective against the fire, nor too high, which could cause damage or injury.

In addition to pumps, aerial ladders mounted on fire trucks exemplify mechanical aptitude in use. These ladders must be extended and manipulated with precision to reach high floors of buildings safely. Firefighters operating these ladders need to calculate angles and extensions accurately based on the building's height and distance from the truck. They must also account for variables such as wind and the weight load on the ladder to maintain stability and safety during operation. Understanding the mechanical principles of leverage and balance is essential here, as improper use could lead to accidents, causing harm to both firefighters and those they are trying to rescue.

Another vital area where mechanical aptitude is critical is in the use of hydraulic rescue tools, commonly known as the 'Jaws of Life.' These tools are used to cut through metal and debris in rescue operations, such as extricating passengers from wrecked vehicles. The operation of these tools involves understanding hydraulic systems, which apply the principles of fluid mechanics to generate enormous forces with relatively little input effort. Firefighters must be adept at quickly assembling and operating these tools, often in confined and chaotic environments, to provide rapid assistance to accident victims.

Ventilation is another firefighting operation that heavily relies on mechanical aptitude. Firefighters often need to ventilate a building during a fire to control the spread of smoke and fire gases, a process that involves creating openings in buildings in strategic locations. This requires not only strength but also an understanding of structural mechanics to determine the most effective points for ventilation without compromising the building's integrity. It also involves knowledge of airflow dynamics to predict how the fire will behave once ventilation changes the fire's environment.

Moreover, mechanical aptitude extends to the maintenance of equipment—a crucial aspect of firefighting preparedness. Firefighting gear, tools, and vehicles undergo regular checks and maintenance to ensure they are ready for immediate use. Firefighters must be familiar with the mechanical aspects of their equipment to perform necessary repairs and maintenance, reducing the likelihood of malfunctions during critical moments. This includes everything from lubricating moving parts to replacing worn components.

Firefighters also apply their mechanical knowledge in managing water supply systems during larger or rural fires where hydrants are not readily available. Setting up temporary water relay systems or drafting water from lakes or pools requires a thorough understanding of suction principles and the mechanics of water flow, ensuring that these improvised solutions are effective when needed.

In training, firefighters are continually honed in their mechanical skills through simulations that replicate real-life scenarios. These training exercises are designed not only to teach the fundamentals of equipment operation but also to ingrain a mechanical intuition that can guide firefighters during the stress and unpredictability of actual fire scenes.

Approaching and solving mechanical reasoning questions

Approaching and solving mechanical reasoning questions effectively requires a thoughtful process, blending critical thinking with a firm grasp of mechanical principles. These types of questions are common in various technical and aptitude tests, including those for firefighting positions, where understanding mechanical concepts is essential for safe and efficient job performance. Developing a methodical approach to these questions helps not only to secure good marks on tests but also to solve practical problems on the job.

When first encountering a mechanical reasoning question, it is crucial to carefully read and analyze the question to understand what is being asked. Many mistakes are made by rushing through this initial step, leading to misunderstandings about the nature of the problem. It's important to identify the key components involved in the question: What exactly are the forces, movements, or mechanical relationships at play? Often, these questions will involve a scenario, such as gears turning, weights being lifted, or objects being thrown, and understanding the scenario in detail is the first step toward crafting a solution.

After thoroughly understanding the question, visualize the mechanical process or draw a simple diagram. This visualization helps in making abstract concepts more concrete and allows for better manipulation of the elements involved. For instance, if the question involves pulleys, drawing the pulleys with the ropes and forces indicated can help clarify how the components interact. This step is critical as it makes the problem-solving process more manageable and structured.

The next step is to apply the relevant mechanical principles. This could involve calculating forces, considering laws of motion, or applying principles of equilibrium. For example, if the question concerns balancing forces on a lever, one would apply the principle of moments, which states that for the system to be in equilibrium, the clockwise moments must equal the anticlockwise moments. Knowing and correctly applying these foundational principles is crucial, as they provide the means to move from a qualitative understanding of the problem to a quantitative solution.

As you perform calculations, it's vital to keep track of units and ensure that they are consistent throughout the problem-solving process. Misalignment of units can lead to errors in calculation, which might result in incorrect answers. If you find yourself stuck on a problem, revisiting the basics and ensuring that all the units match up can often help clarify where the issue lies.

An effective strategy in solving these questions is also to consider edge cases or simplify the problem. For example, if dealing with a complex system of gears, considering what happens when one gear turns a single revolution might simplify the understanding of the entire system's movement. Simplification can help break down a complex problem into more manageable parts, each of which can be solved step by step.

Always double-check your work, especially your calculations and logic. In mechanical reasoning, as in real-world mechanical applications, small errors can lead to significantly incorrect outcomes. Reviewing your steps to ensure that each phase of your reasoning is sound not only enhances accuracy but also builds confidence in your solutions.

Time management is another critical aspect when approaching these questions, particularly in a testing scenario. While it is important to be thorough, spending too much time on one difficult question can jeopardize your ability to complete the test. Practice with timed quizzes and tests can help develop a sense of how much time to allocate to each question and when it might be better to move on and return to a tricky problem later.

In addition to these strategies, continual practice is essential. Regularly engaging with mechanical reasoning questions helps refine your approach and enhances your ability to apply mechanical principles quickly and accurately. Many resources are available, including textbooks, online courses, and practice tests, which provide a wide range of examples and can help build a deep reservoir of experience to draw from during tests.

Ultimately, the skills developed in approaching and solving mechanical reasoning questions have direct implications beyond passing tests. In firefighting, for instance, these skills translate into better problem-solving in emergency situations, where understanding and manipulating mechanical systems can save lives and protect property. This synthesis of academic preparation and practical application underscores the value of mastering mechanical reasoning, making it a key competency in many technical fields.

CHAPTER 4

NAVIGATING SITUATIONAL JUDGMENT

Decision-Making Under Pressure

The significance of situational judgment for firefighters

Situational judgment tests (SJTs) are increasingly used in the selection and training processes for firefighters, reflecting their crucial role in assessing a candidate's practical decision-making skills and behavioral tendencies in work-related scenarios. These tests present candidates with realistic, hypothetical scenarios that they are likely to encounter on the job and ask them to choose the best response from a set of options. The primary goal of situational judgment tests is to evaluate a candidate's ability to make sound decisions quickly and effectively, which is paramount in the high-stakes environment of firefighting.

The significance of situational judgment for firefighters cannot be overstated. Firefighting involves complex, dynamic environments where decisions often have to be made under pressure and with incomplete information. These decisions can have profound implications, not only for the safety and effectiveness of the firefighting team but also for the public and the community they serve. Situational judgment tests help ensure that those entering this critical field are equipped with the necessary cognitive and emotional skills to handle these challenges effectively.

In these tests, scenarios are carefully designed to mirror the types of situations firefighters might face. These can range from managing interpersonal conflicts within the team, responding to emergencies involving hazardous materials, making tactical decisions during a rapidly evolving fire, or interacting with the public in stressful situations. Each scenario is structured to assess how well candidates understand the priorities and values important to firefighting, such as safety, communication, teamwork, and public service.

The responses in SJTs are evaluated based on a framework that reflects the best practices and protocols of firefighting. These frameworks are developed through extensive consultations with firefighting professionals and are grounded in the realities of the job. The most effective responses typically demonstrate a balance between decisive action and adherence to safety protocols, highlighting the candidate's ability to weigh various factors and make a decision that optimizes outcomes while minimizing risks.

For instance, a situational judgment test might present a scenario where a firefighter must choose between saving a visibly endangered life immediately or securing a potentially unstable structure first. The correct answer would depend on various factors specific to the scenario, such as the immediate risk to the firefighter and others, the likelihood of the structure's collapse, and the potential for additional casualties. Such questions test the candidate's ability to assess risk, prioritize actions, and make decisions that reflect both courage and caution.

Moreover, SJTs are valuable not only for assessing what decisions candidates make but also for how they make those decisions. Some tests delve deeper by asking candidates to rate the effectiveness of different actions or to explain their reasoning. This provides further insight into their problem-solving process, ethical considerations, and ability to anticipate the consequences of their actions.

The use of SJTs in assessing potential firefighters also extends to predicting long-term job performance and suitability. Research has shown that performance in situational judgment tests can correlate with later job performance, particularly in roles that require interpersonal communication, adaptive thinking, and ethical judgment. By selecting candidates who score well on these tests, fire departments can improve overall team effectiveness and reduce the likelihood of issues such as conflict, misconduct, or poor crisis management.

In addition to their role in selection, situational judgment tests are also used as training tools within fire departments. By exposing trainees to a wide range of scenarios and possible responses, these tests help develop firefighters' decision-making skills in a controlled, reflective environment. This training can encourage firefighters to think critically about their instincts and habits, refine their judgment, and prepare them better for the unpredictability of real-world firefighting.

Exam format and types of scenarios presented.

The situational judgment section of a firefighter's exam is crucial for assessing a candidate's readiness to handle the complex, high-pressure situations they will face on the job. This part of the exam is structured to closely mimic the kinds of decisions firefighters must make in real emergencies and during typical workdays, involving a variety of scenarios that range from operational tactics to ethical dilemmas and interpersonal interactions.

In the format of this exam section, candidates are typically presented with a series of detailed scenarios described in a narrative form. Each scenario is designed to be reflective of real-life situations, and candidates are required to respond by selecting an action from multiple choices provided or by ranking the possible actions from most to least appropriate. This method is particularly effective in gauging a candidate's practical application of their knowledge, their ability to think critically under pressure, and their judgment in balancing various factors such as safety, protocol adherence, and the welfare of the public and their team.

Scenarios in the situational judgment tests are varied to cover the broad scope of challenges a firefighter might encounter. For instance, candidates may face a scenario where they are first on the scene of a multi-vehicle collision with potential fire hazards and multiple injuries. The description would detail the scene, including specific hazards, the apparent condition of the victims, traffic conditions, and available resources. Candidates might then choose the best immediate action to secure the area, manage bystanders, prioritize victims for treatment based on their injuries, and determine how best to deploy their team and equipment.

Another common scenario could involve handling internal team conflicts. Here, the situation might describe a heated dispute between team members over the best approach to tackling a complex fire in a high-risk area, such as a chemical plant. Candidates would need to assess the situation and decide how to intervene in the argument, considering the need to act quickly while ensuring that all team members feel heard and respected.

Resource management scenarios are also frequent, where candidates need to decide how to allocate limited firefighting resources during a day with multiple simultaneous calls. These scenarios require candidates to analyze the severity of each situation, potential risks, and the resources required for each incident to make strategic decisions that optimize the safety and effectiveness of their responses.

Ethical dilemmas are particularly telling in these exams, as they reveal much about a candidate's moral framework. A scenario might present a situation where a candidate finds that a colleague has bypassed safety protocols during an emergency, potentially putting the team at risk. The candidate would need to weigh the implications of their response, considering team safety, the seriousness of the protocol breach, and the importance of trust and accountability within the team.

Public interaction scenarios test a candidate's ability to manage relations with civilians during emergencies. A scenario could involve dealing with an aggressive individual who is obstructing emergency operations, requiring the candidate to use communication skills to defuse the situation effectively and maintain public safety without escalating tensions.

Safety protocol scenarios are essential for testing a candidate's adherence to and understanding of critical safety measures. For example, they might be asked to outline their steps when called to a scene involving dangerous chemicals, testing their knowledge of hazardous material handling and the precautions necessary to protect themselves, their team, and the public.

The analysis of responses in these scenarios focuses not just on the actions chosen but also on the reasoning behind them. High-scoring responses generally demonstrate a candidate's ability to integrate technical knowledge with a sound judgment strategy, prioritize under pressure, and maintain a balanced approach that upholds the core values of the firefighting profession.

Preparing for this section of the exam does more than prepare candidates for testing; it prepares them for real-world service, where the ability to assess complex situations and make informed, ethical, and effective decisions can literally save lives and property. The situational judgment test is, therefore, not just an exam component—it's a vital training ground for the critical thinking and decision-making skills that define the best in the firefighting profession.

Understanding Situational Judgment

Framework for effective decision-making

Understanding situational judgment and developing a framework for effective decision-making is crucial for individuals in roles that demand quick, responsible, and informed choices under pressure. This capability is especially significant in fields such as firefighting, where the consequences of decisions can have immediate and profound impacts on safety and outcomes. Developing a solid framework for situational judgment not only aids in making effective decisions but also ensures these decisions are consistent, reproducible, and justifiable, which is paramount in maintaining trust and authority in critical situations.

Situational judgment involves assessing a scenario in all its complexity, recognizing the underlying challenges, and deciding the best course of action based on a combination of analysis, experience, and ethical considerations. To excel in situational judgment, one must not only have a deep understanding of the specific technical knowledge required for their role but also an adeptness at critical thinking, emotional intelligence, and a strong ethical foundation.

The first step in forming a framework for effective decision-making is to develop a thorough understanding of the environment and the specifics of each situation. This means gathering as much information as possible to assess the scenario accurately. In the context of firefighting, this could involve understanding the type of fire, the layout of the building, the materials involved, and the presence of civilians. Information gathering is critical as it forms the base upon which all further decisions are made.

Once the situation is understood, the next step is to define the objectives clearly. What are the immediate goals? In firefighting, the primary objectives are typically to ensure the safety of civilians and firefighters, followed by extinguishing the fire and preventing further damage. Clear objectives help in prioritizing actions and can guide decision-making throughout the response to the situation.

After setting the objectives, the next step is to consider the resources available. What personnel, equipment, and information are at your disposal? How can these resources be best utilized to achieve the objectives? Understanding the resources available helps in planning actions that are within the realm of possibility and avoids overcommitting, which can lead to failures and mishaps.

The fourth step involves analyzing the potential options for action. Each option should be evaluated for its feasibility, risks, and potential outcomes. This analysis should be comprehensive, considering both the short-term and long-term implications of each decision. In high-pressure environments like firefighting, decision-makers often use decision matrices or similar tools to weigh the consequences of different actions against their potential benefits.

A critical part of situational judgment is anticipation. Effective decision-makers have the ability to anticipate possible future scenarios based on their actions. This foresight can prevent choices that lead to dead ends or exacerbate the situation. Anticipation is a skill developed through experience and rigorous training; it involves pattern recognition, understanding of cause and effect, and deep knowledge of the specific context in which one is operating.

Once a course of action is decided upon, implementation must be swift and decisive. However, effective decision-making also involves monitoring the results of the action and being prepared to adjust the approach if the situation changes or the expected outcomes are not achieved. This flexibility to adapt to evolving conditions is crucial in dynamic environments.

Moreover, after the situation is resolved, a critical review of the decision-making process is invaluable. This review should involve all stakeholders and include an honest assessment of what was successful and what could have been done better. Learning from each situation enhances future decision-making capabilities and can lead to improvements in processes and outcomes.

Ethical considerations are also a fundamental part of situational judgment. Decisions should be made with a strong adherence to ethical guidelines and standards. In many professions, especially those that impact public safety, like firefighting, maintaining ethical integrity is crucial not only for the effectiveness of the response but also for public trust and respect.

Analyzing the situation: What you need to consider

Analyzing a situation effectively is crucial in any professional context but becomes critically important in fields like emergency response, where decisions need to be both quick and well-informed to ensure safety and efficiency. In such high-stakes environments, the ability to break down a situation and assess various elements accurately can significantly impact the outcomes.

When faced with a complex situation, several layers need to be peeled back and examined. Each layer represents different aspects of the situation that can influence the decision-making process. It starts from the initial observation and moves through deeper analysis to uncover not just the obvious details but also the subtler dynamics at play.

The first step in analyzing any situation is to gather as much information as possible. This involves observing the immediate environment and understanding the visible elements. For instance, a firefighter arriving at a scene will first notice the size of the fire, the type of building involved, and any signs of victims or bystanders. However, effective analysis requires not only taking in what is immediately apparent but also seeking out less obvious information that might be crucial. This might involve checking for the presence of hazardous materials, understanding the building's layout, and assessing weather conditions that could influence the behavior of the fire.

Once the basic information is collected, the next step is to prioritize the information based on urgency and importance. Prioritization helps in managing cognitive load, allowing professionals to focus on the most pressing issues first without becoming overwhelmed by less critical details. In emergency scenarios, this often means prioritizing human life and safety above all else. For instance, ensuring that all inhabitants are evacuated from a building may take precedence over beginning to combat a fire.

Context is another critical component of situation analysis. Context involves understanding the situation within a broader framework. This might include considering the time of day, which affects visibility and the likely presence of people in the area; historical data about similar situations and their outcomes; or local regulations that might impact how the situation should be handled. For example, fighting a fire in a commercial area during working hours poses different challenges and risks than in a residential area at night.

Analyzing risk is an integral part of situational analysis. Risk assessment involves evaluating the potential dangers associated with different actions and determining which risks are acceptable and which are not. It also involves contingency planning for worst-case scenarios. In firefighting, this might mean assessing the risk of a building collapsing and ensuring that all personnel are aware of escape routes and safe zones.

Resource assessment is also crucial. This involves evaluating what resources are available, how they can be best used, and what limitations might affect the response. Resources include personnel, equipment, information, and time. Effective situation analysis accounts for resource constraints and looks for ways to optimize resource use. For example, if there are limited water supplies at a fire scene, firefighters might need to use more targeted methods to control the fire or call for additional support.

Communication also plays a vital role in situation analysis. In many professional settings, especially those involving teams, the ability to communicate clearly and effectively can greatly influence the outcome. For emergency responders, this means not only communicating internally among the team but also with other agencies, the public, and possibly victims. Effective communication ensures that all parties have the necessary information to make informed decisions and remain coordinated.

After considering all these factors, synthesizing the information is the final step in analyzing a situation. This involves bringing together all the data, priorities, risks, and resources into a coherent understanding of what is happening and what needs to be done. This synthesis should lead to a strategic plan of action that addresses the most critical aspects of the situation first.

Responding to Emergencies

Prioritizing actions under time constraints

Responding to emergencies effectively requires a nuanced understanding of how to prioritize actions under time constraints. This capability is especially crucial in professions like firefighting, emergency medical services, and law enforcement, where the speed and order of decisions can significantly impact outcomes. Prioritizing correctly ensures that the most critical tasks are addressed first, potentially saving lives and minimizing damage.

In emergency situations, every second counts. The ability to quickly assess a situation and determine the most pressing needs is vital. Prioritization during emergencies involves a dynamic evaluation of what actions will provide the most significant benefit or mitigate the most substantial risk at any given moment. This assessment is continually updated as the situation evolves.

The initial step in responding to an emergency is to ensure personal and team safety. This foundational principle guides all emergency response efforts; rescuers must secure their own safety and that of their team to effectively assist others. For instance, firefighters are trained to assess the structural integrity of a burning building before entering. They need to ensure that they are not putting themselves in undue danger, as becoming victims themselves would only escalate the emergency.

Once safety is secured, the next priority is typically to stabilize the situation to prevent it from worsening. This can involve a variety of actions depending on the nature of the emergency. In a medical emergency, it might mean performing CPR on a person who is not breathing. In a fire scenario, it could involve containing the fire to prevent it from spreading to adjacent structures. Stabilizing the situation provides a more controlled environment in which to carry out further actions and can often help to limit the ultimate scope of the emergency.

Following stabilization, the focus shifts to systematic mitigation efforts—actions aimed at reducing the immediate effects of the emergency. This might involve rescuing individuals from dangerous situations, providing critical medical treatment, or suppressing a fire. These actions are often resource-intensive and require careful coordination. Effective mitigation is dependent on the groundwork laid by earlier prioritization and stabilization efforts, allowing responders to maximize their impact.

Communication is a critical component throughout the emergency response process. Prioritizing communication ensures that all team members and external agencies involved are informed and aligned in their efforts. This includes not only disseminating orders and information but also gathering feedback and intelligence from various sources. Effective communication can significantly enhance the efficiency and effectiveness of the response, ensuring that resources are deployed where they are most needed.

Throughout the emergency response, decision-makers must continuously assess and reassess their priorities. What was a priority one moment may become less critical as the situation evolves. For example, once a fire is contained, the priority may shift from active suppression to evacuation and medical care for affected individuals. This dynamic prioritization requires responders to be flexible and adaptive, traits that are honed through training and experience.

Another aspect of responding to emergencies is the post-emergency analysis. After the immediate threat has been addressed, it is crucial to prioritize debriefing and learning from the incident. This stage often involves reviewing the actions taken during the emergency, identifying what worked well and what did not, and adjusting protocols and training accordingly. This reflective practice not only helps improve future responses but also reinforces the importance of prioritization and systematic action under pressure.

The principles of prioritizing actions under time constraints are universally applicable across various types of emergencies. Whether dealing with natural disasters, medical emergencies, fires, or public safety incidents, the ability to quickly determine and address the most pressing needs can make a profound difference in the outcomes. Emergency responders are trained extensively in these skills, which involve both an intuitive understanding of emergencies and a methodical approach to decision-making. These skills are continually refined through simulations, real-world experiences, and the study of past emergency responses.

Explanation of ideal responses and common mistakes

In high-pressure scenarios, such as those faced by emergency responders, the ability to provide ideal responses can be the difference between success and failure. Understanding what constitutes an ideal response and recognizing common mistakes are essential components of effective emergency management. Whether dealing with fires, medical crises, or natural disasters, clarity in actions and decisions can significantly influence outcomes.

An ideal response in emergency situations typically involves a series of well-considered actions that are both effective and efficient. These actions are predicated on a thorough assessment of the situation, utilizing a systematic approach that prioritizes safety, resource management, and the specific goals of the scenario. Each step of an ideal response is backed by training, protocols, and an intuitive understanding of the situation, honed through experience and continuous learning.

The foundation of an ideal response begins with an accurate and rapid assessment of the situation. This initial evaluation is crucial as it informs all subsequent decisions. Responders must quickly identify the key elements of the scenario—what the immediate danger is, who is at risk, what resources are available, and what actions will produce the most favorable outcome. This requires a clear understanding of the environment, the ability to interpret signs and symptoms, and the knowledge to apply appropriate solutions.

Following the assessment, the next step in an ideal response is the formulation of a clear and actionable plan. This plan should outline a series of steps that address the most critical aspects of the emergency first. For instance, in a medical emergency, this might mean securing the airway, stopping bleeding, or preventing shock before addressing less critical injuries. In a fire, it involves ensuring the safety of individuals and then containing and extinguishing the fire.

Effective communication throughout the process is also a hallmark of an ideal response. Clear, concise, and direct communication not only between team members but also with victims, bystanders, and other agencies involved is essential. Proper communication ensures that all parties are informed of the situation and their roles, which coordinates efforts and minimizes confusion and errors.

Moreover, an ideal response adapts as the situation evolves. Flexibility and the ability to reassess and adjust the plan based on new information or changing conditions are vital. Effective emergency responders are those who can pivot their strategies as required without losing sight of the ultimate goal—resolving the situation with minimal harm and maximum efficiency.

However, even with the best training and intentions, mistakes can occur. Common mistakes in emergency responses often stem from a failure to adequately assess the situation. This can lead to misjudging the severity of the scenario or missing critical details that could inform better decision-making. For example, a responder might underestimate the potential for a fire to spread due to hidden combustible materials or overestimate the stability of a structure that has been compromised.

Another frequent error is poor communication. This might manifest as unclear instructions, failure to listen to team members or other agencies, or insufficient updates as the situation progresses. Communication failures can lead to duplication of efforts, resources being misdirected, or, in the worst case, increased risk of injury or death.

Additionally, a lack of flexibility can be detrimental in dynamic emergency environments. Adhering too rigidly to a preconceived plan without considering evolving conditions can prevent responders from adapting to the actual needs of the situation. This might lead to ineffective solutions that do not address the root problems or changing dynamics of the emergency.

Ineffective resource management is another common pitfall. This can occur if resources are not used strategically or if there is a failure to prioritize tasks effectively. Inefficient use of resources can deplete crucial supplies and personnel, leaving responders unable to maintain a sustained effort where needed.

To mitigate these mistakes, ongoing training is essential. Simulation exercises and continuous education help responders practice and refine their skills in controlled environments where they can learn from errors without real-world consequences. Debriefing after an actual emergency is also crucial. These sessions should involve a candid discussion of what went well and what did not, allowing teams to learn from each experience and improve their future responses.

Dear Readers,

Thank you for making it halfway through our Firefighter Exam Prep Guide! We hope the content so far has been both educational and empowering as you continue your journey toward becoming a firefighter. If you find this guide helpful, please consider leaving a review on Amazon. Your feedback not only supports our work but also aids other aspiring firefighters in navigating their exam preparation.

How You Can Share Your Review:

Through Amazon.com:

1. Go to the Amazon page where you found my book.
2. Navigate to the 'Customer Reviews' section.
3. Click on 'Write a customer review' to share your valuable insights.

Instant QR Code Access: Simply scan the QR code below with your smartphone to be directed to the Amazon review section.

CHAPTER 5

SPATIAL ORIENTATION EXPERTISE

Mapping Success

The role of spatial awareness in firefighting.

Spatial awareness plays a critical role in firefighting, a profession where understanding and navigating complex environments under extreme conditions can significantly impact the effectiveness and safety of fire suppression efforts. Firefighters rely heavily on spatial awareness to assess situations rapidly, make strategic decisions, and execute operations that save lives and protect property. This skill is not just about knowing locations and layouts; it's about interpreting and reacting to dynamic, often hazardous environments where visibility is low, risks are high, and conditions change rapidly.

At the core of firefighting operations is the need to understand the physical space of any incident scene. Firefighters must quickly grasp the layout of buildings, the location of fire hydrants, and the potential spread patterns of the fire. This immediate need to map their environment mentally allows firefighters to navigate effectively inside burning structures, locate victims, and position equipment optimally. For instance, knowing the layout of a multi-story building helps firefighters determine the fastest and safest routes for evacuation and hose advancement, which can drastically affect the outcome of their operations.

Spatial awareness also encompasses the ability to judge distances and spaces accurately, which is crucial when working in environments that are smoke-filled or structurally compromised. Firefighters must be able to estimate the distance between themselves and various points of interest, like exits or fire sources, even in poor visibility. This ability ensures they can move quickly and efficiently without getting disoriented, which is critical in avoiding injuries or fatalities during operations.

Moreover, spatial awareness extends to understanding the relationship between different elements within the environment. Firefighters must assess how different building materials will react to heat, anticipate how fire will spread through various pathways like vents or open doors, and identify structural weaknesses that may lead to collapses. This understanding allows them to predict and counteract the fire's behavior, strategically ventilating buildings to control the direction and intensity of flames and smoke, thus creating safer conditions for both firefighting personnel and trapped occupants.

The role of spatial awareness in firefighting is not only reactive but also proactive. During planning and prevention activities, firefighters use spatial data to analyze fire risks in communities, plan the placement of new fire stations, and develop pre-incident plans for high-risk buildings. These activities require a detailed understanding of geographic and structural layouts to optimize response times and effectiveness. For example, using maps and building blueprints, firefighters can pre-plan their entry points and hose deployment strategies, which can be crucial during actual fire incidents.

In training, spatial awareness is honed through simulations and live exercises that replicate real-world scenarios. Firefighting trainees practice navigating through smoke-filled environments, learn to use thermal imaging cameras to see through smoke and engage in search and rescue operations in maze-like structures. These training exercises are designed to enhance their ability to interpret and navigate spaces quickly and accurately, preparing them for the unpredictable and dynamic nature of real fire scenes.

The development of spatial awareness is also supported by technological tools and resources. Modern firefighting equipment includes GPS systems, drones, and advanced imaging technologies such as infrared and thermal cameras. These tools help firefighters gain a comprehensive view of the incident scene, enhancing their spatial understanding and decision-making capabilities. For instance, drones can be used to provide aerial views of a fire, helping command units visualize the overall scene and make informed decisions about resource deployment and tactical approaches.

Overview of the spatial orientation section.

The Spatial Orientation section of an exam is an essential component in assessing a candidate's capability to comprehend and manipulate three-dimensional space and relationships, a skill that is particularly vital in fields requiring precise navigation and handling of spatial data, such as firefighting, aviation, and certain engineering disciplines. This section aims to evaluate an individual's ability to visualize objects from different angles, understand maps and diagrams, and effectively solve spatial problems that mirror real-world tasks.

Candidates taking this section can expect a series of challenges that test various aspects of spatial reasoning. Typically, these challenges are presented through diagrams, maps, and graphical representations, which require a keen understanding of spatial concepts. This section delves deep into one's ability to interpret complex visual information and make accurate judgments about spatial relationships.

One of the key areas tested is the ability to visualize objects when rotated or flipped. Candidates may encounter questions that present an object in a specific orientation, and then they may be asked to identify how that object would look from another angle or if it were rotated along an axis. This tests the mental ability to maintain object constancy despite changes in perspective, a skill crucial for professions that deal with three-dimensional objects or environments regularly.

Another significant aspect of the Spatial Orientation section is navigation and map reading skills. This involves interpreting geographic information systems, building layouts, or city maps. Questions might simulate scenarios where a candidate needs to determine the fastest or safest route between two points or locate objects and landmarks based on directional and locational clues. Such skills are indispensable for emergency responders who must navigate quickly and efficiently in unfamiliar settings under pressure.

Perspective-taking questions challenge candidates to adopt different viewpoints and predict what can be seen from those perspectives. For example, a candidate might be shown a complex layout or structure from a bird's eye view and asked what would be visible from ground level at a certain point. This ability to shift perspectives is critical for tasks such as planning rescue operations in multi-story buildings or operating machinery where components are not directly visible.

Understanding spatial relationships forms another crucial component of this test section. Candidates might be asked to identify how different elements in a space relate to one another. For instance, understanding the arrangement of rooms in a building based solely on a floor plan or deducing the position of various components within a machine. Accurately interpreting these relationships helps in the effective planning and execution of tasks that depend on the layout of physical spaces.

Lastly, the section may include challenges that involve three-dimensional problem-solving. These problems require the manipulation of 3D shapes and objects in one's mind, such as figuring out how different parts fit together to form a complex object or determining the volume of space an object will occupy. These types of questions assess a candidate's ability to deal with physical dimensions in planning and problem-solving scenarios.

Preparing for this exam section involves more than just understanding theoretical concepts; it requires practical engagement with spatial tasks. Activities that can enhance spatial reasoning include practicing with models or virtual simulation tools, engaging in games that require strategic movement and placement, and studying technical drawings or architectural plans.

Fundamental Concepts of Spatial Orientation

Understanding maps, diagrams, and spatial relationships

Spatial orientation is a fundamental cognitive skill that involves understanding one's position in space relative to the surrounding environment and navigating through it. This capability is crucial in many fields, particularly those requiring navigation, planning, and interaction with spatial constructs, such as architecture, engineering, urban planning, and emergency response, including firefighting and rescue operations. The core concepts of spatial orientation include understanding maps, interpreting diagrams, and comprehending spatial relationships, each integral to effectively navigating and manipulating one's environment.

Understanding maps is perhaps the most visible aspect of spatial orientation. Maps are scaled representations of physical spaces that provide critical information about geographical locations, distances, and features within a given area. The ability to read and interpret maps allows individuals to navigate between locations, plan routes, and strategize movements, especially in unfamiliar terrains. For instance, a firefighter uses maps to identify the quickest routes to a fire incident, locate nearby water sources, and understand the layout of the area to coordinate effective emergency responses.

Maps contain various symbols and notations that require interpretation. For example, topographic maps show the terrain and elevation of an area using contour lines. Understanding these symbols allows users to visualize the three-dimensional layout of the terrain from a two-dimensional perspective. This skill is crucial for planning in fields such as construction and land development and is equally important in outdoor activities like hiking or military operations where navigation over varied terrains is necessary.

Diagrams, another critical component, are simplified drawings intended to show the layout, structure, or workings of something, often with specific parts labeled. In the context of spatial orientation, diagrams help to abstract more complex realities into understandable visuals. For firefighters, this might involve interpreting building floor plans or system schematics to quickly locate critical infrastructure like gas valves or electrical systems during an emergency. Similarly, an engineer might use circuit diagrams to troubleshoot or design complex systems. The ability to interpret diagrams accurately is, therefore, essential for correctly implementing or modifying designs and for ensuring safety and efficiency during operations.

Spatial relationships refer to how objects are placed in space in relation to each other. Understanding spatial relationships involves comprehending various properties such as distance, direction, proximity, and hierarchy. This can involve anything from determining whether one room in a building plan is accessible from another without passing through a third room to understanding how changes to one part of a system might affect another. In practical applications, spatial relationships help with tasks such as assembling machinery, planning the layout of a room, or efficiently organizing materials in a warehouse.

To truly grasp these concepts, engaging in activities that enhance spatial reasoning skills is often required. This might involve exercises like orienteering, which combines map reading with physical navigation, or using simulation software that allows for virtual interaction with three-dimensional models. Activities that challenge the understanding and manipulation of space, such as puzzles like Rubik's Cube or strategic games like chess, can also sharpen one's ability to think spatially.

Education plays a crucial role in developing spatial orientation skills. In academic settings, subjects like geometry directly engage with spatial concepts through the study of shapes, sizes, and the properties of space. In professional environments, targeted training programs can help individuals refine their ability to interpret maps and diagrams relevant to their specific fields. For example, pilots undergo rigorous training in reading aviation charts and navigational systems as part of their certification process.

In today's digital age, technology also significantly enhances our ability to understand and interact with space. Geographic Information Systems (GIS) provide powerful tools for visualizing and analyzing spatial data, allowing for more informed decision-making in urban planning, environmental management, and public safety. Virtual reality (VR) and augmented reality (AR) technologies offer immersive ways to experience and manipulate spatial information, providing valuable tools for education and training in various fields.

Visual and Spatial Problem Solving

Strategies for tackling orientation and visualization questions

Visual and spatial problem-solving skills are essential in many disciplines, from architecture and engineering to emergency services and visual arts. These skills enable individuals to interpret visual information accurately, manipulate objects mentally, and solve problems that involve physical spaces or visual representations. Developing effective strategies for tackling orientation and visualization questions is therefore crucial for anyone looking to enhance their cognitive toolkit in these areas.

One of the foundational strategies in visual and spatial problem-solving is the development of strong visualization skills. This involves the ability to create a mental image of an object or scene and to manipulate that image in the mind without the aid of physical tools. For example, an architect visualizing a building project might mentally rotate the structure to consider how different light angles will affect the building's interior at various times of the day. Similarly, a firefighter might mentally map a burning building to plan the safest entry and exit routes. Enhancing these visualization skills can be achieved through practice exercises such as mentally rotating shapes or objects, which is often part of spatial ability tests.

Another effective strategy is the use of diagrams and sketches to solve spatial problems. Visual representations can simplify complex information, making it easier to analyze and manipulate. For instance, drawing diagrams can help solve physics problems that involve forces and motion, and sketching a layout can assist in planning an art installation or a public event. Diagrams provide a visual shorthand that can make complex relationships and data more comprehensible, thereby aiding decision-making and problem-solving.

Breaking down complex problems into smaller, manageable parts is also a critical strategy in visual and spatial problem-solving. This approach, often referred to as decomposition, involves analyzing a large problem by separating it into its constituent elements. For instance, when tackling a complex engineering problem, an engineer might break it down into individual components like structure, function, and connectivity. Each component can then be solved individually, simplifying the overall problem-solving process. This method not only makes the problem less overwhelming but also allows for a more detailed focus on each aspect, increasing the accuracy of the solution.

Employing analogical reasoning is another valuable strategy. This involves using knowledge from a familiar context to solve a new problem with similar underlying structures. For example, understanding how water flows through pipes can help in understanding how electricity flows in circuits, as both can be described by similar principles of flow and resistance. Analogies can provide powerful insights and shortcuts in problem-solving by transferring existing knowledge to new and unfamiliar contexts.

Additionally, using transformation techniques can be a powerful approach to visual and spatial problem-solving. This strategy involves altering the physical or visual representation of a problem to make its solution more evident. For instance, transforming a three-dimensional problem into a two-dimensional diagram can often reveal underlying patterns and relationships that were not initially apparent. Techniques such as scaling, rotating, and translating are useful tools in this context, helping to change perspectives and potentially simplify the problem-solving process.

Collaboration often brings multiple perspectives to a visual or spatial problem, making it easier to find innovative solutions. Collaborative problem-solving takes advantage of the diverse visual and spatial reasoning styles of different individuals, potentially leading to more creative and effective solutions. For instance, in a design team, one member might excel at generating conceptual visualizations, while another might be better at detailed spatial analysis, together providing a comprehensive approach to solving design challenges.

Finally, practicing with real-world tasks can significantly enhance visual and spatial problem-solving abilities. Engaging in activities that require these skills, such as assembling furniture, playing video games that involve navigation and spatial planning, or participating in sports that require good spatial awareness, such as golf or soccer, can improve one's ability to visualize and orient within spaces effectively.

Tips for interpreting and navigating through complex layouts

Navigating through complex layouts and interpreting intricate visual and spatial information are skills that are essential across a spectrum of fields, from architecture and urban planning to emergency response and graphic design. Whether maneuvering through a densely packed city, orchestrating the layout of an upcoming art gallery exhibition, or strategizing an emergency exit route from a large building, the ability to effectively manage complex spatial information is invaluable. Here, practical advice is provided to enhance these skills, facilitating smoother navigation and interpretation of complicated environments.

One of the first steps in handling complex layouts is to develop a clear understanding of the space. This can be achieved by studying maps, blueprints, or diagrams of the area before attempting navigation. For instance, firefighters often review building plans as part of their pre-incident planning, allowing them to familiarize themselves with potential entry points and hazards. Similarly, event planners might study venue diagrams to optimize the flow and placement of guests, equipment, and displays. Taking time to review these materials in advance can prevent confusion and errors during actual navigation.

Another effective strategy is to break down the space into smaller, manageable sections. This method, known as segmentation, simplifies navigation by reducing a large complex area into more understandable parts. For example, a large office building can be divided by floors or wings, with each section being analyzed individually for exits, stairwells, and key features. This approach not only makes the task less daunting but also enhances the accuracy of spatial understanding, as focusing on smaller areas allows for more detailed attention.

Utilizing technology is another crucial aspect of interpreting and navigating complex layouts. Modern tools such as GPS applications, augmented reality (AR), and virtual reality (VR) can provide real-time assistance and visual overlays that guide users through complex spaces. In urban navigation, GPS apps offer turn-by-turn directions that help individuals navigate complex city layouts efficiently. Similarly, AR can be used in museums or historical sites to provide visitors with interactive maps and directional cues through their mobile devices, enriching their experience and aiding navigation.

Visual cues play a significant role in effective navigation. When planning to navigate through complex layouts, one should note unique landmarks, color-coded paths, or signage that can serve as guides. In large facilities like hospitals or airports, wayfinding systems are often designed with distinct visual symbols or color schemes for different areas, helping visitors and staff orient themselves and navigate the space more intuitively.

Practicing spatial relationships is also key to mastering complex layouts. This involves understanding how different parts of a space relate to each other and how movement in one area affects positioning relative to other areas. Engaging in activities that require spatial reasoning, such as puzzle solving or playing strategy games, can enhance one's ability to perceive and manage these relationships effectively.

Effective communication is essential, especially when navigating complex spaces, which involve coordinating with others. Clear, concise descriptions of locations, directions, and landmarks are crucial for ensuring that all individuals involved can understand and follow the planned routes. This is particularly important in emergency situations where precise and rapid communication can determine the success of evacuation or rescue operations.

Furthermore, maintaining situational awareness is critical when dealing with complex spatial environments. This means being continuously aware of one's surroundings and being able to adjust plans as circumstances change. Situational awareness involves not only paying attention to the layout but also monitoring the presence of other people, potential obstacles, and changing conditions within the environment.

Lastly, regular practice and exposure to different types of complex layouts will naturally improve one's ability to navigate and interpret these spaces. Regular visits to new cities, participation in orienteering sports, or exploration of different architectural styles and building designs can all serve as practical ways to enhance spatial awareness and navigational skills.

CHAPTER 6

PRACTICAL QUESTIONS AND ANSWERS

Reading Comprehension Practical Questions

Passage 1:

The cheetah is known for being the fastest land animal, capable of reaching speeds up to 60 miles per hour in short bursts covering distances up to 500 meters. This incredible speed is due to its long, powerful legs, large nasal passages, and a flexible spine.

1: What feature primarily contributes to the cheetah's ability to run fast?

A) Its small size
B) Its large paws
C) Its flexible spine
D) Its sharp claws

2: How far can a cheetah cover in a short burst?

A) 100 meters
B) 500 meters
C) 200 meters
D) 60 meters

3: What is the top speed a cheetah can reach?

A) 30 miles per hour
B) 40 miles per hour
C) 50 miles per hour
D) 60 miles per hour

4: What anatomical feature of the cheetah aids in its high speed?

A) Short legs
B) Large paws
C) Small nasal passages
D) Long, powerful legs

5: Why can cheetahs only maintain their top speed for short distances?

A) They tire quickly
B) They overheat
C) They lose balance
D) Their muscles cramp

Passage 2:

Solar panels convert sunlight into electricity using photovoltaic cells. They work best on sunny days but can still generate some power on cloudy days. Proper installation, which includes the optimal angle and direction, can significantly improve their efficiency.

6: What do solar panels use to convert sunlight into electricity?

A) Solar batteries
B) Photovoltaic cells
C) Thermal cells
D) Electric grids

7: When do solar panels work best?

A) On rainy days
B) On sunny days
C) On cloudy days
D) At night

8: What can significantly improve the efficiency of solar panels?

A) Painting them black
B) Cleaning them daily
C) Proper installation
D) Using larger panels

9: Can solar panels generate power on cloudy days?

A) Yes
B) No

10: What aspect of installation is important for solar panel efficiency?

A) The color of the panels
B) The brand of the panels
C) The angle and direction
D) The size of the panels

Passage 3:

Honeybees play a critical role in pollination, which is essential for the reproduction of many plants. They collect nectar and pollen, which they use to produce honey. This process not only provides food for the bees but also benefits humans by aiding in crop production.

11: What role do honeybees play in the environment?

A) They produce silk
B) They help in pollination
C) They provide shade
D) They eat pests

12: What do honeybees collect to produce honey?

A) Leaves
B) Seeds
C) Nectar and pollen
D) Bark

13: Why is pollination essential?

A) For the growth of trees
B) For the reproduction of plants
C) For soil fertilization
D) For water conservation

14: How do honeybees benefit humans?

A) By controlling insect populations
B) By producing honey
C) By creating nests
D) By making wax

15: What is the main food source for honeybees?

A) Fruits
B) Nectar
C) Small insects
D) Leaves

Passage 4:

Mount Everest, the highest mountain in the world, stands at 29,032 feet above sea level. It attracts climbers from all over the globe, though it poses significant challenges such as extreme weather, altitude sickness, and difficult terrain.

16: What is Mount Everest known for?

A) Being the most dangerous mountain
B) Being the highest mountain
C) Having the most wildlife
D) Having the easiest trails

17: How high is Mount Everest?

A) 28,000 feet
B) 29,032 feet
C) 30,000 feet
D) 31,000 feet

18: What is one of the challenges climbers face on Mount Everest?

A) Easy terrain
B) Mild weather
C) Altitude sickness
D) Abundant food sources

19: Why do climbers from all over the world go to Mount Everest?

A) To study its wildlife
B) To experience its beauty
C) To conquer the highest peak
D) To collect samples

20: What makes Mount Everest challenging besides its height?

A) Lack of wildlife
B) Extreme weather
C) Lack of trails
D) Poor visibility

Passage 5:

Photosynthesis is the process by which green plants use sunlight to synthesize foods with the help of chlorophyll. This process converts carbon dioxide and water into glucose and oxygen, providing the essential energy that plants need to grow.

21: What do plants use to carry out photosynthesis?

A) Oxygen
B) Carbon monoxide
C) Chlorophyll
D) Nitrogen

22: What are the products of photosynthesis?

A) Water and carbon dioxide
B) Glucose and oxygen
C) Nitrogen and glucose
D) Oxygen and hydrogen

23: What role does sunlight play in photosynthesis?

A) It cools the plants
B) It provides energy for the process
C) It provides nutrients
D) It helps absorb water

24: Why is photosynthesis important for plants?

A) It produces seeds
B) It synthesizes foods for growth
C) It helps them breathe
D) It repels insects

25: What is one of the inputs required for photosynthesis?

A) Glucose
B) Oxygen
C) Carbon dioxide
D) Soil

Passage 6:

The Great Wall of China, one of the most impressive architectural feats in history, stretches over 13,000 miles. Originally built to protect Chinese states from invasions, it now stands as a testament to China's historical strength and perseverance.

26: What was the original purpose of the Great Wall of China?

A) To serve as a trade route
B) To display architectural skills
C) To protect against invasions
D) To mark territorial boundaries

27: How long is the Great Wall of China?

A) 5,000 miles
B) 10,000 miles
C) 13,000 miles
D) 15,000 miles

28: What does the Great Wall symbolize today?

A) Modern architecture
B) China's military power
C) Historical strength and perseverance
D) Ancient trade routes

29: What type of structure is the Great Wall of China?

A) A monument
B) A fort
C) A wall
D) A temple

30: What historical period does the Great Wall of China primarily represent?

A) Modern China
B) Ancient China
C) The Industrial Revolution
D) The Ming Dynasty

Passage 7:

The invention of the printing press by Johannes Gutenberg in the 15th century revolutionized the spread of information. It made books more accessible, reduced costs, and contributed to the rise in literacy rates across Europe.

31: Who invented the printing press?

A) Isaac Newton
B) Galileo Galilei
C) Johannes Gutenberg
D) Leonardo da Vinci

32: What century was the printing press invented?

A) 12th century
B) 15th century
C) 18th century
D) 20th century

33: What was one significant impact of the printing press?

A) Decreased book production
B) Increased book costs
C) Improved accessibility to books
D) Reduced literacy rates

34: How did the printing press affect literacy rates in Europe?

A) It decreased them
B) It had no effect
C) It increased them
D) It caused illiteracy

35: What was a consequence of the printing press on the spread of information?

A) Information spread more slowly
B) Information became more accessible
C) Information became more expensive
D) Information was limited to the elite

Passage 8:

The development of antibiotics in the early 20th century marked a significant milestone in medical history. These drugs, which combat bacterial infections, have saved countless lives and revolutionized the treatment of diseases such as tuberculosis and pneumonia.

36: What do antibiotics combat?

A) Viral infections
B) Fungal infections
C) Bacterial infections
D) Genetic disorders

37: When were antibiotics developed?

A) 18th century
B) 19th century
C) Early 20th century
D) Late 20th century

38: Name a disease that antibiotics have helped treat.

A) Cancer
B) Tuberculosis
C) Diabetes
D) Heart disease

39: What was a major impact of the development of antibiotics?

A) Reduced medical costs
B) Revolutionized the treatment of diseases
C) Increased bacterial resistance
D) Decreased use of other medications

40: How have antibiotics affected human health?

A) They have saved countless lives
B) They have increased the occurrence of diseases
C) They have had no impact
D) They have caused new infections

Passage 9:

The Mona Lisa, painted by Leonardo da Vinci, is one of the most famous pieces of art in the world. This portrait, known for its enigmatic expression, attracts millions of visitors to the Louvre Museum in Paris each year.

41: Who painted the Mona Lisa?

A) Vincent van Gogh
B) Pablo Picasso
C) Leonardo da Vinci
D) Claude Monet

42: Where is the Mona Lisa displayed?

A) The British Museum
B) The Louvre Museum
C) The Metropolitan Museum of Art
D) The Prado Museum

43: What is the Mona Lisa known for?

A) Its large size
B) Its vibrant colors
C) Its enigmatic expression
D) Its abstract style

44: How many visitors does the Mona Lisa attract each year?

A) Thousands
B) Hundreds
C) Millions
D) Dozens

45: In which city is the Louvre Museum located?

A) Rome
B) London
C) Paris
D) Madrid

Passage 10:

The invention of the airplane by the Wright brothers in 1903 marked the beginning of modern aviation. Their success at Kitty Hawk demonstrated that controlled, sustained flight was possible, paving the way for the future of air travel.

46: Who invented the airplane?

A) The Wright brothers
B) The Montgolfier brothers
C) Thomas Edison
D) Alexander Graham Bell

47: When did the Wright brothers achieve their first successful flight?

A) 1890
B) 1903
C) 1910
D) 1920

48: Where did the Wright brothers' first successful flight take place?

A) Dayton
B) Kitty Hawk
C) New York
D) Chicago

49: What did the Wright brothers' invention demonstrate?

A) The possibility of space travel
B) The feasibility of controlled, sustained flight
C) The limits of human flight
D) The design of modern airports

50: What industry did the Wright brothers' invention pave the way for?

A) Automobile
B) Railway
C) Aviation
D) Maritime

Passage 11:

Marie Curie's pioneering research on radioactivity won her two Nobel Prizes in Physics and Chemistry. Her discoveries not only advanced the field of science but also laid the groundwork for the development of X-ray machines.

51: What did Marie Curie research?

A) Electromagnetism
B) Radioactivity
C) Thermodynamics
D) Genetics

52: How many Nobel Prizes did Marie Curie win?

A) One
B) Two
C) Three
D) Four

53: In which fields did Marie Curie win her Nobel Prizes?

A) Medicine and Literature
B) Physics and Chemistry
C) Biology and Physics
D) Chemistry and Medicine

54: What significant medical technology was developed based on Curie's discoveries?

A) MRI machines
B) Ultrasound
C) X-ray machines
D) CT scanners

55: What was one impact of Marie Curie's discoveries?

A) They halted scientific research
B) They advanced the field of science
C) They were kept secret
D) They led to environmental degradation

Passage 12:

Neil Armstrong, an American astronaut, became the first person to walk on the moon on July 20, 1969. His famous words, "That's one small step for man, one giant leap for mankind," have been etched in history, symbolizing human achievement in space exploration.

56: Who was the first person to walk on the moon?

A) Yuri Gagarin
B) Buzz Aldrin
C) Michael Collins
D) Neil Armstrong

57: When did Neil Armstrong walk on the moon?

A) 1965
B) 1967
C) 1969
D) 1971

58: What were Neil Armstrong's famous words when he stepped on the moon?

A) "To infinity and beyond"
B) "The eagle has landed"
C) "That's one small step for man, one giant leap for mankind"
D) "Houston, we have a problem"

59: What does Neil Armstrong's moonwalk symbolize?

A) The end of the space race
B) Human achievement in space exploration
C) The start of space tourism
D) The failure of moon missions

60: What nationality was Neil Armstrong?

A) Russian
B) American
C) British
D) Canadian

Passage 13:

William Shakespeare, widely regarded as one of the greatest playwrights in history, authored numerous plays and sonnets that have been celebrated for their intricate plots, rich characters, and profound themes. His works, including "Hamlet," "Macbeth," and "Romeo and Juliet," continue to be performed and studied worldwide.

61: Who is considered one of the greatest playwrights in history?

A) Charles Dickens
B) William Shakespeare
C) Jane Austen
D) Mark Twain

62: Which of the following is a work by Shakespeare?

A) "Great Expectations"
B) "Pride and Prejudice"
C) "Hamlet"
D) "Moby-Dick"

63: What are Shakespeare's works known for?

A) Simple language
B) Intricate plots
C) Historical accuracy
D) Modern settings

64: Which play was written by Shakespeare?

A) "War and Peace"
B) "Macbeth"
C) "Ulysses"
D) "The Great Gatsby"

65: What is a common theme in Shakespeare's works?

A) Technological advancements
B) Profound themes about human nature
C) Exploration of the Americas
D) Political satire

Passage 14:

The discovery of penicillin by Alexander Fleming in 1928 marked a turning point in medical history. This antibiotic revolutionized the treatment of bacterial infections, leading to the development of numerous other antibiotics and saving countless lives.

66: Who discovered penicillin?

A) Louis Pasteur
B) Alexander Fleming
C) Robert Koch
D) Edward Jenner

67: When was penicillin discovered?

A) 1918
B) 1928
C) 1938
D) 1948

68: What type of medical treatment did penicillin revolutionize?

A) Viral infections
B) Genetic disorders
C) Bacterial infections
D) Parasitic diseases

69: What was the impact of penicillin's discovery?

A) It increased the cost of medical treatments
B) It revolutionized the treatment of bacterial infections
C) It decreased the use of antibiotics
D) It had no significant impact

70: What did the discovery of penicillin lead to?

A) The development of vaccines
B) The development of other antibiotics
C) The invention of surgical tools
D) The discovery of DNA

Passage 15:

The Taj Mahal, built by Emperor Shah Jahan in memory of his wife Mumtaz Mahal, stands as a symbol of love and architectural beauty. This white marble mausoleum, located in Agra, India, is renowned for its intricate artistry and harmonious proportions.

71: Who built the Taj Mahal?

A) Akbar the Great
B) Shah Jahan
C) Aurangzeb
D) Babur

72: Why was the Taj Mahal built?

A) As a palace
B) As a fortress
C) In memory of Shah Jahan's wife
D) To mark a victory

73: Where is the Taj Mahal located?

A) New Delhi
B) Mumbai
C) Jaipur
D) Agra

74: What material is the Taj Mahal primarily made of?

A) Granite
B) Sandstone
C) White marble
D) Limestone

75: What is the Taj Mahal renowned for?

A) Its modern design
B) Its military significance
C) Its intricate artistry and harmonious proportions
D) Its political history

Passage 16:

The Grand Canyon, carved by the Colorado River, is one of the most famous natural landmarks in the United States. Its vast and colorful landscape reveals millions of years of geological history, attracting millions of tourists each year.

76: What natural feature carved the Grand Canyon?

A) Wind
B) Glaciers
C) Colorado River
D) Earthquakes

77: What does the Grand Canyon reveal?

A) Human history
B) Geological history
C) Biological evolution
D) Ancient civilizations

78: Where is the Grand Canyon located?

A) California
B) Arizona
C) Nevada
D) Utah

79: Why do millions of tourists visit the Grand Canyon each year?

A) To see the wildlife
B) To explore ancient ruins
C) To view its vast and colorful landscape
D) To participate in water sports

80: What makes the Grand Canyon famous?

A) Its dense forests
B) Its ancient temples
C) Its geological formations
D) Its urban development

Passage 17:

The Hubble Space Telescope, launched in 1990, has provided humanity with stunning images and invaluable data about the universe. Orbiting outside Earth's atmosphere, it avoids atmospheric distortion and captures detailed observations of distant stars, galaxies, and other celestial phenomena.

81: When was the Hubble Space Telescope launched?

A) 1980
B) 1990
C) 2000
D) 2010

MATHEMATICAL REASONING PRACTICAL QUESTIONS

1: What is the value of 2+2×3?

A) 8
B) 12
C) 6
D) 10

2: Solve for x if 5x−3=2x+12.

A) 3
B) 5
C) 6
D) 7

3: If a train travels 60 miles in 1.5 hours, what is its average speed in miles per hour?

A) 30
B) 40
C) 45
D) 50

4: Simplify $\frac{15}{25}$.

A) $\frac{2}{3}$
B) $\frac{3}{5}$
C) $\frac{5}{6}$
D) $\frac{4}{5}$

5: What is the area of a rectangle with a length of 5 units and a width of 3 units? A=L(W)

A) 15 square units
B) 20 square units
C) 8 square units
D) 12 square units

6: If x=3, what is the value of $2x^2-4x+1$?

A) 11
B) 12
C) 13
D) 14

7: What is the solution to the equation 2x+5=17?

A) 5
B) 6
C) 4
D) 3

8: How many degrees are in the sum of the interior angles of a triangle?

A) 90
B) 180
C) 270
D) 360

9: Solve for y: 3y−2=7.

A) 2
B) 3
C) 4
D) 5

10: What is the value of 5^2-3^2?

A) 16
B) 20
C) 8
D) 10

11: If the radius of a circle is 4 units, what is the circumference? (Use π≈3.14) $2\pi r$

A) 12.56 units
B) 18.84 units
C) 25.12 units
D) 31.4 units

12: What is $\frac{3}{4}$ of 20?

A) 10
B) 12
C) 15
D) 18

13: If a car travels 150 miles on 5 gallons of gas, how many miles per gallon does it get?

A) 25
B) 30
C) 20
D) 35

14: Simplify 2x×3x.

A) 5^2
B) 6^2
C) 6x
D) 5x

15: What is the value of $\sqrt{49}$?

A) 6
B) 7
C) 8
D) 9

16: If a=4 and b=2, what is the value of 3a−b?

A) 10
B) 8
C) 14
D) 6

17: Solve for z: 4z+6=18.

A) 2
B) 3
C) 4
D) 5

18: What is 10% of 200?

A) 10
B) 20
C) 30
D) 40

19: If a rectangle has a perimeter of 24 units and one side is 6 units, what is the length of the other side?

A) 6
B) 8
C) 10
D) 12

20: Simplify $\frac{24}{36}$.

A) $\frac{2}{3}$ ✓
B) $\frac{3}{4}$
C) $\frac{3}{5}$
D) $\frac{2}{5}$

21: Solve for x: 7x−5=16.

A) 3
B) 4
C) 5
D) 6

22: What is the value of 8^2?

A) 48
B) 56
C) 64
D) 72

23: If the base of a triangle is 6 units and its height is 4 units, what is the area?

A) 12 square units
B) 14 square units
C) 24 square units
D) 18 square units

24: Convert 0.75 to a fraction. ∧ 100

A) $\frac{3}{4}$
B) $\frac{2}{3}$
C) $\frac{1}{2}$
D) $\frac{3}{5}$

25: Solve for y: 2y+4=12.

A) 3
B) 4
C) 5
D) 6

26: What is the value of 4^3?

A) 48
B) 56
C) 64
D) 72

27: Simplify $\frac{18}{24}$.

A) $\frac{3}{4}$
B) $\frac{2}{3}$
C) $\frac{5}{6}$
D) $\frac{3}{5}$

28: If x=2, what is the value of x^3-3x?

A) 4
B) 2
C) 1
D) 0

29: Solve for x: 3x+4=19.

A) 4
B) 5
C) 6
D) 7

30: What is the perimeter of a square with a side length of 5 units?

A) 10 units
B) 15 units
C) 20 units
D) 25 units

31: Convert 25% to a fraction.

A) $\frac{1}{2}$
B) $\frac{1}{4}$
C) $\frac{1}{3}$
D) $\frac{1}{5}$

32: What is the value of 9^2?

A) 72
B) 81
C) 64
D) 100

33: If the diameter of a circle is 10 units, what is the radius?

A) 2 units
B) 4 units
C) 5 units
D) 6 units

34: Solve for y: 5y−2=3y+8.

A) 3
B) 5
C) 6
D) 7

35: What is the value of $\sqrt{81}$?

A) 7
B) 8
C) 9
D) 10

36: Simplify $\frac{28}{42}$.

A) $\frac{2}{3}$
B) $\frac{3}{4}$
C) $\frac{3}{5}$
D) $\frac{2}{5}$

37: What is the area of a circle with a radius of 7 units? (Use π≈3.14)

A) 153.86 square units
B) 154.86 square units
C) 155.86 square units
D) 156.86 square units

38: Solve for z: 6z+9=33.

A) 3
B) 4
C) 5
D) 6

39: What is the value of $\frac{1}{2} \times 12$?

A) 5
B) 6
C) 7
D) 8

40: If a triangle has sides of 3 units, 4 units, and 5 units, what type of triangle is it?

A) Equilateral
B) Isosceles
C) Scalene
D) Right

41: Solve for x: 4x−7=9.

A) 2
B) 3
C) 4
D) 5

42: What is the volume of a cube with side length of 3 units?

A) 9 cubic units
B) 12 cubic units
C) 27 cubic units
D) 36 cubic units

43: Convert 0.6 to a fraction.

A) $\frac{3}{5}$
B) $\frac{1}{2}$
C) $\frac{2}{3}$
D) $\frac{3}{4}$

44: What is the value of $7^2 + 2^2$?

A) 49
B) 53
C) 65
D) 58

45: Solve for y: 4y−5=11.

A) 3
B) 4
C) 5
D) 6

46: Simplify $\frac{45}{60}$.

A) $\frac{1}{2}$

B) $\frac{2}{3}$

C) $\frac{3}{4}$

D) $\frac{3}{5}$

47: If x=5, what is the value of x^2-4x+3?

A) 6

B) 7

C) 8

D) 9

48: Solve for z: 5z+10=35.

A) 3

B) 4

C) 5

D) 6

49: What is 20% of 150?

A) 20

B) 30

C) 40

D) 50

50: What is the circumference of a circle with a diameter of 8 units? (Use π≈3.14)

A) 18.84 units

B) 21.84 units

C) 22.84 units

D) 25.12 units

51: Solve for x: 2x+7=15.

A) 2

B) 3

C) 4

D) 5

52: What is the value of 6^2?

A) 30

B) 36

C) 42

D) 48

53: Simplify $\frac{32}{40}$.

A) $\frac{3}{4}$

B) $\frac{2}{3}$

C) $\frac{4}{5}$

D) $\frac{5}{6}$

54: Convert 0.2 to a fraction.

A) $\frac{1}{2}$

B) $\frac{1}{3}$

C) $\frac{1}{4}$

D) $\frac{1}{5}$

55: What is the area of a rectangle with length 8 units and width 4 units?

A) 24 square units
B) 30 square units
C) 32 square units
D) 36 square units

56: Solve for y: 3y+6=21.

A) 4
B) 5
C) 6
D) 7

57: What is the value of 10^2-5^2?

A) 25
B) 50
C) 75
D) 100

58: What is the volume of a rectangular prism with length 4 units, width 3 units, and height 2 units?

A) 20 cubic units
B) 24 cubic units
C) 30 cubic units
D) 36 cubic units

59: Convert 50% to a fraction.

A) $\frac{1}{2}$
B) $\frac{1}{3}$
C) $\frac{1}{4}$
D) $\frac{1}{5}$

60: What is the value of 333^333?

A) 9
B) 18
C) 27
D) 36

61: Simplify $\frac{14}{21}$.

A) $\frac{3}{2}$
B) $\frac{3}{4}$
C) $\frac{3}{5}$
D) $\frac{2}{5}$

62: If the base of a triangle is 8 units and its height is 5 units, what is the area?

A) 20 square units
B) 30 square units
C) 40 square units
D) 50 square units

63: Solve for x: 9x−4=32.

A) 3
B) 4
C) 5
D) 6

64: What is the value of √64?

A) 6
B) 7
C) 8
D) 9

65: If a=3 and b=5, what is the value of 2a+3b?

A) 19
B) 20
C) 21
D) 22

66: What is the value of 5^3?

A) 50
B) 75
C) 100
D) 125

67: Solve for z: 8z+12=52.

A) 4
B) 5
C) 6
D) 7

68: What is 25% of 80?

A) 15
B) 20
C) 25
D) 30

69: What is the perimeter of a rectangle with length 10 units and width 6 units?

A) 26 units
B) 30 units
C) 32 units
D) 36 units

70: Convert 0.5 to a fraction.

A) $\frac{1}{3}$
B) $\frac{1}{4}$
C) $\frac{1}{5}$
D) $\frac{1}{2}$

71: What is the value of 2^4?

A) 8
B) 12
C) 16
D) 20

72: Simplify $\frac{48}{60}$.

A) $\frac{2}{3}$
B) $\frac{4}{5}$
C) $\frac{3}{5}$
D) $\frac{3}{4}$

73: Solve for y: 7y+2=23.

A) 2
B) 3
C) 4
D) 5

74: What is the value of $\sqrt{36}$?

A) 4
B) 5
C) 6
D) 7

75: What is the volume of a cylinder with radius 3 units and height 5 units? (Use π≈3.14)

A) 141.3 cubic units
B) 142.3 cubic units
C) 143.3 cubic units
D) 144.3 cubic units

76: What is the area of a square with side length 6 units?

A) 36 square units
B) 40 square units
C) 42 square units
D) 48 square units

77: Convert 0.4 to a fraction.

A) $\frac{1}{3}$
B) $\frac{1}{4}$
C) $\frac{1}{5}$
D) $\frac{2}{5}$

78: Solve for x: 3x+4=25.

A) 6
B) 7
C) 8
D) 9

79: What is the value of 8^2?

A) 64
B) 72
C) 80
D) 88

80: Simplify $\frac{21}{28}$.

A) $\frac{2}{3}$
B) $\frac{3}{4}$
C) $\frac{3}{5}$
D) $\frac{2}{5}$

81: What is 15% of 200?

A) 20
B) 25
C) 30
D) 35

MECHANICAL REASONING PRACTICAL QUESTIONS

1: Which tool is used to measure the internal diameter of a pipe?

A) Caliper
B) Micrometer
C) Ruler
D) Protractor

2: What type of lever is a seesaw?

A) First class
B) Second class
C) Third class
D) Fourth class

3: In a pulley system, what is the main advantage?

A) Increases speed
B) Reduces effort
C) Decreases distance
D) Enhances balance

4: What device converts electrical energy into mechanical energy?

A) Generator
B) Transformer
C) Motor
D) Battery

5: What type of gear has teeth that are straight and parallel to the axis?

A) Helical gear
B) Bevel gear
C) Spur gear
D) Worm gear

6: What is the function of a flywheel in an engine?

A) To increase friction
B) To store energy
C) To reduce noise
D) To filter air

7: How does an inclined plane reduce the effort needed to lift a load?

A) Increases distance
B) Reduces friction
C) Decreases angle
D) Increases speed

8: What is the mechanical advantage of a lever with a 5-meter effort arm and a 1-meter load arm?

A) 1
B) 5

C) 10
D) 0.5

9: Which component in a car reduces friction between moving parts?

A) Brake
B) Bearing
C) Axle
D) Clutch

10: What does a hydraulic system use to transmit force?

A) Air
B) Water
C) Oil
D) Electricity

11: In a first-class lever, where is the fulcrum located?

A) Between the load and effort
B) At the load end
C) At the effort end
D) Near the effort

12: What is the purpose of a ratchet mechanism?

A) To change direction of force
B) To allow rotation in one direction only
C) To increase speed
D) To reduce noise

13: Which simple machine consists of a wheel with a rope or belt around it?

A) Lever
B) Pulley
C) Inclined plane
D) Screw

14: How does a screw convert rotational motion into linear motion?

A) By using threads
B) By using a wheel
C) By using a lever
D) By using a pulley

15: What type of energy is stored in a compressed spring?

A) Kinetic
B) Potential
C) Thermal
D) Electrical

16: What does a camshaft do in an engine?

A) Stores fuel
B) Regulates the timing of the valves
C) Converts electrical energy
D) Increases speed

17: How does a gear train change the direction of force?

A) By altering speed
B) By meshing gears with different orientations
C) By using a lever
D) By using a belt

18: What type of gear is used to transmit motion between intersecting shafts?

A) Spur gear
B) Helical gear
C) Bevel gear
D) Worm gear

19: What is the principle behind a hydraulic press?

A) Archimedes' principle
B) Bernoulli's principle
C) Pascal's law
D) Boyle's law

20: What type of pulley system reduces the effort needed to lift a load by half?

A) Single fixed pulley
B) Single movable pulley
C) Double fixed pulley
D) Double movable pulley

21: How does a wedge work?

A) By increasing surface area
B) By converting rotational force
C) By separating objects
D) By reducing friction

22: What is the main function of a crankshaft in an engine?

A) To store fuel
B) To convert linear motion to rotational motion
C) To filter air
D) To reduce noise

23: What type of mechanical linkage converts linear motion into rotational motion?

A) Camshaft
B) Crankshaft
C) Flywheel
D) Gear train

24: Which part of an engine controls the intake and exhaust of air-fuel mixture?

A) Piston
B) Camshaft
C) Crankshaft
D) Carburetor

25: How does a differential gear in a car work?

A) By transmitting torque evenly
B) By allowing wheels to rotate at different speeds
C) By increasing speed
D) By reducing noise

26: What is the function of an alternator in a vehicle?

A) To convert mechanical energy into electrical energy
B) To store fuel
C) To increase speed
D) To reduce noise

27: What type of motion does a piston in an engine perform?

A) Circular
B) Rotational
C) Linear
D) Oscillating

28: Which tool is used to tighten or loosen bolts with a specific torque?

A) Wrench
B) Screwdriver
C) Torque wrench
D) Pliers

29: What does a tachometer measure?

A) Speed of a vehicle
B) Torque of an engine
C) Rotational speed of an engine
D) Pressure in a cylinder

30: How does a centrifugal pump move fluid?

A) By using a piston
B) By using a diaphragm
C) By using centrifugal force
D) By using a screw

31: What is the purpose of a gasket in an engine?

A) To increase speed
B) To filter air
C) To prevent leakage
D) To reduce noise

32: How does a thermostat in a car engine work?

A) By measuring speed
B) By regulating temperature
C) By increasing pressure
D) By reducing noise

33: What is the function of a radiator in a vehicle?

A) To store fuel
B) To cool the engine
C) To increase speed
D) To reduce noise

34: What does a belt drive do in a mechanical system?

A) Transmits power between pulleys
B) Converts rotational motion to linear motion
C) Increases speed
D) Reduces friction

35: How does a hydraulic jack lift heavy loads?

A) By using a lever
B) By using hydraulic pressure
C) By using an inclined plane
D) By using a pulley

36: What type of bearing reduces friction between a rotating shaft and a fixed housing?

A) Thrust bearing
B) Journal bearing
C) Needle bearing
D) Ball bearing

37: What is the main purpose of a fuse in an electrical circuit?

A) To increase voltage
B) To store energy
C) To protect against overcurrent
D) To convert energy

38: How does an anemometer measure wind speed?

A) By using a pressure gauge
B) By using rotating cups
C) By using a thermometer
D) By using a barometer

39: What does a voltmeter measure?

A) Current
B) Voltage
C) Resistance
D) Power

40: How does a transformer change voltage levels?

A) By converting DC to AC
B) By using induction
C) By using a capacitor
D) By increasing current

41: What is the principle of operation for a lever?

A) Bernoulli's principle
B) Pascal's law
C) Archimedes' principle
D) Principle of moments

42: What type of lever is a wheelbarrow?

A) First class
B) Second class

C) Third class
D) Fourth class

43: How does a mechanical advantage increase with a lever?

A) By increasing load arm
B) By decreasing effort arm
C) By increasing effort arm
D) By reducing friction

44: What is the function of a cam in mechanical systems?

A) To store energy
B) To regulate the motion of a follower
C) To reduce noise
D) To increase friction

45: How does a gear ratio affect speed in a gear train?

A) Higher ratio increases speed
B) Lower ratio increases speed
C) Higher ratio decreases speed
D) Ratio has no effect on speed

46: What is the purpose of a clutch in a vehicle?

A) To store fuel
B) To engage and disengage power transmission
C) To increase speed
D) To reduce noise

47: How does a pressure gauge work?

A) By measuring temperature
B) By measuring force
C) By measuring electrical resistance
D) By measuring fluid pressure

48: What type of motion does a pendulum exhibit?

A) Linear
B) Circular
C) Oscillating
D) Rotational

49: What is the function of a valve in a hydraulic system?

A) To increase speed
B) To control the flow of fluid
C) To store energy
D) To reduce friction

50: How does a worm gear differ from other gears?

A) It has straight teeth
B) It has helical teeth
C) It transmits motion at right angles
D) It has a screw-like thread

51: What is the function of a piston ring in an engine?

A) To store fuel
B) To seal the combustion chamber
C) To increase speed
D) To reduce noise

52: How does a barometer measure atmospheric pressure?

A) By using mercury
B) By using a thermometer
C) By using a voltmeter
D) By using a hydrometer

53: What is the purpose of a relay in an electrical circuit?

A) To increase current
B) To control a high-power circuit with a low-power signal
C) To store energy
D) To convert energy

54: How does a simple gear train work?

A) By using pulleys
B) By meshing gears of different sizes
C) By using levers
D) By converting electrical energy

55: What type of motion does a crank handle provide?

A) Linear
B) Rotational
C) Oscillating
D) Vibrational

56: What is the main function of an air filter in an engine?

A) To store fuel
B) To remove impurities from the air
C) To increase speed
D) To reduce noise

57: How does a centrifugal clutch work?

A) By using springs
B) By using hydraulic pressure
C) By using centrifugal force
D) By using gears

58: What is the function of a drive shaft in a vehicle?

A) To store fuel
B) To transmit torque from the engine to the wheels
C) To reduce noise
D) To increase speed

59: How does a magnetic compass work?

A) By using an electric current
B) By using the Earth's magnetic field
C) By using a pressure gauge
D) By using a thermometer

60: What type of bearing allows linear motion?

A) Ball bearing
B) Roller bearing
C) Linear bearing
D) Needle bearing

61: What is the principle of operation for a hydraulic lift?

A) Archimedes' principle
B) Bernoulli's principle
C) Pascal's law
D) Boyle's law

62: How does a brake system in a car work?

A) By increasing speed
B) By converting kinetic energy to heat
C) By storing energy
D) By reducing friction

63: What is the purpose of a flywheel in a mechanical system?

A) To store rotational energy
B) To reduce noise
C) To increase speed
D) To convert energy

64: How does a pneumatic system transmit power?

A) By using hydraulic fluid
B) By using compressed air
C) By using electricity
D) By using a lever

65: What is the main function of a gearbox?

A) To increase noise
B) To store fuel
C) To change speed and torque
D) To reduce friction

66: How does a bevel gear work?

A) By using straight teeth
B) By using helical teeth
C) By transmitting motion between intersecting shafts
D) By using a worm thread

67: What is the function of a torque converter in a vehicle?

A) To store fuel
B) To increase speed
C) To transmit and multiply torque
D) To reduce noise

68: How does a diaphragm pump operate?

A) By using a piston
B) By using a rotating wheel
C) By using a diaphragm that moves back and forth
D) By using centrifugal force

69: What is the purpose of a fuse in an electrical circuit?

A) To increase current
B) To store energy
C) To protect against overcurrent
D) To convert energy

70: How does a hydraulic press work?

A) By using a lever
B) By using hydraulic fluid to exert force
C) By using an inclined plane
D) By using a pulley

71: What type of energy does a capacitor store?

A) Kinetic
B) Potential
C) Thermal
D) Electrical

72: How does a friction clutch work?

A) By using hydraulic pressure
B) By using compressed air
C) By using friction between surfaces
D) By using magnetic fields

73: What is the function of a camshaft in an engine?

A) To store fuel
B) To regulate the timing of the valves
C) To increase speed
D) To reduce noise

74: How does a worm gear work?

A) By using straight teeth
B) By using helical teeth
C) By transmitting motion at right angles
D) By using a screw-like thread

125

75: What is the main purpose of a gasket in an engine?

A) To increase speed
B) To filter air
C) To prevent leakage
D) To reduce noise

76: How does a tachometer measure rotational speed?

A) By measuring torque
B) By using a pressure gauge
C) By counting rotations per minute
D) By using a thermometer

77: What type of motion does a piston in an engine perform?

A) Circular
B) Rotational
C) Linear
D) Oscillating

78: What is the function of an alternator in a vehicle?

A) To convert mechanical energy into electrical energy
B) To store fuel
C) To increase speed
D) To reduce noise

79: How does a diaphragm pump operate?

A) By using a piston
B) By using a rotating wheel
C) By using a diaphragm that moves back and forth
D) By using centrifugal force

80: What is the main function of a gearbox?

A) To increase noise
B) To store fuel
C) To change speed and torque
D) To reduce friction

81: How does a pneumatic system transmit power?

A) By using hydraulic fluid
B) By using compressed air
C) By using electricity
D) By using a lever

SITUATIONAL JUDGMENT PRACTICAL QUESTIONS

Situation 1:

You are a firefighter responding to a house fire. Upon arrival, you notice heavy smoke coming from the windows, and a woman is frantically screaming that her child is still inside.

1. What is your first priority upon arriving at the scene?

A) Ensure the woman is safe and away from the fire
B) Start fighting the fire immediately
C) Perform a risk assessment and plan a rescue operation
D) Call for additional backup

2. While assessing the situation, you notice the fire is spreading rapidly. What should you do next?

A) Wait for backup to arrive
B) Enter the building immediately to rescue the child
C) Use a fire extinguisher to try and control the fire
D) Ensure the safety of your team and the surrounding area

3. The woman is hysterical and trying to run back into the house. How do you handle her?

A) Let her go inside if she insists
B) Physically restrain her from entering
C) Calmly explain the danger and assure her you are handling the situation
D) Ignore her and focus on the fire

4. Your team enters the building and finds the child unconscious but breathing. What is the next step?

A) Continue searching the house for more victims
B) Carry the child outside to safety
C) Begin CPR immediately
D) Call for medical assistance from inside the house

5. After rescuing the child, you notice a propane tank near the fire. What should you do?

A) Move the tank to a safe distance
B) Inform your team and evacuate the area
C) Try to extinguish the fire around the tank

D) Leave the tank and continue fighting the fire elsewhere

Situation 2:

You are a new firefighter in your team and have just completed your probationary period. One of your colleagues seems to be ignoring safety protocols during training exercises.

6. What should be your first step in addressing this situation?

A) Confront your colleague directly and ask them to follow the protocols
B) Report the behavior to your supervisor immediately
C) Ignore it, assuming they know what they are doing
D) Discuss your concerns with another team member

7. If your colleague dismisses your concerns, what should you do next?

A) Let it go and focus on your own tasks
B) Continue to remind them about the protocols
C) Document their behavior and report it to your supervisor
D) Try to cover for their mistakes to avoid conflict

8. During a team meeting, the supervisor asks if anyone has any concerns about safety. What should you do?

A) Stay quiet to avoid causing trouble
B) Bring up your colleague's behavior as a general safety concern
C) Talk to the supervisor privately after the meeting
D) Wait for someone else to speak up

9. Your colleague's behavior has not changed, and it is affecting the team's performance. How do you proceed?

A) Take over their tasks to ensure they are done correctly
B) Request a transfer to another team
C) Continue to monitor the situation and report any incidents
D) Confront your colleague more aggressively

10. What is the most important reason to address this behavior?

A) To maintain team discipline
B) To ensure the team's safety during emergencies
C) To show your leadership skills
D) To avoid getting in trouble with your supervisor

Situation 3:

You are on a rescue mission in a multi-story building during a severe earthquake. There are reports of multiple people trapped on different floors, and the structure is unstable.

11. What is your first action upon entering the building?

A) Start searching the nearest rooms for survivors
B) Assess the structural integrity of the building
C) Go directly to the top floor where most people are trapped
D) Wait for further instructions from your team leader

12. You find a group of people on the second floor who need help. What should you do next?

A) Help them evacuate immediately
B) Continue searching for more people
C) Report their location to your team leader
D) Leave them and focus on reaching the top floor

13. One of your teammates is trapped under debris. How do you handle the situation?

A) Continue the mission and come back for them later
B) Stop everything and rescue your teammate first
C) Call for backup and assist in freeing them
D) Assign another team member to stay with them

14. You hear cries for help from a higher floor, but the stairway is blocked. What is your next step?

A) Try to clear the blockage immediately
B) Find an alternative route to reach them
C) Wait for specialized equipment to arrive
D) Focus on rescuing those on the lower floors

15. During the rescue, the building starts to shake again. What should you do?

A) Evacuate everyone immediately
B) Find a safe spot and wait until it stops
C) Continue with the rescue operation
D) Move to a more stable part of the building

Situation 4:

You are at a community event where your fire department has set up a booth to educate the public about fire safety. A child approaches you, very curious about firefighting, and asks many questions about the equipment and your job.

16. How should you respond to the child's curiosity?

A) Give short, factual answers to their questions
B) Ignore the child and focus on other visitors
C) Engage with the child and explain as much as possible
D) Redirect the child to another firefighter

17. The child asks if they can try on your helmet. What should you do?

A) Let them try it on under your supervision
B) Tell them it's not allowed and move on
C) Give it to them and walk away
D) Ignore the request and continue talking

18. A parent joins the conversation and asks about fire safety tips for their home. How do you respond?

A) Provide general fire safety tips and offer to visit their home for a check
B) Give them a brochure and walk away
C) Tell them to look up information online
D) Avoid answering and focus on the child

19. A group of teenagers starts playing with the fire extinguisher display. What should you do?

A) Ignore them and hope they stop
B) Tell them to stop and explain the importance of the equipment
C) Call security to remove them

D) Let them continue as long as they are not causing damage

20. An elderly person asks you about fire escape plans. What is the best way to help them?

A) Explain the steps to create a fire escape plan and provide a brochure
B) Tell them to call the fire department for more information
C) Give them a quick answer and move on
D) Ignore the question and focus on other visitors

Situation 5:

During a training session, you notice that the equipment you are using is malfunctioning. This could potentially lead to accidents if not addressed immediately.

21. What should you do first when you notice the malfunctioning equipment?

A) Continue using it and hope it doesn't cause problems
B) Stop using it and report the issue to your supervisor
C) Try to fix it yourself without informing anyone
D) Ignore it and let others deal with it

22. Your supervisor is not available. What is your next step?

A) Use the equipment carefully until your supervisor returns
B) Inform another senior team member about the issue
C) Leave the training session and wait for your supervisor
D) Continue with the training using the faulty equipment

23. A fellow firefighter suggests ignoring the malfunction and completing the training. How do you respond?

A) Agree and continue using the equipment
B) Insist on reporting the issue and stop using the equipment
C) Argue with them about safety protocols
D) Leave the training session

24. You decide to stop using the equipment and report the issue. What information should you provide?

A) Only mention that the equipment is broken
B) Describe the malfunction in detail and its potential risks
C) Say that you don't want to use the equipment anymore

D) Provide your opinion on how to fix it

25. The training supervisor thanks you for reporting the issue. How should you proceed?

A) Wait for the supervisor to fix the equipment
B) Suggest alternative training methods while the equipment is being repaired
C) Leave the training session
D) Ask for a break until the equipment is fixed

Situation 6:

You are a senior firefighter and notice that a new team member is struggling with the physical demands of the job. They are having difficulty keeping up during training exercises.

26. What should be your first step in addressing this situation?

A) Ignore the issue and hope they improve
B) Offer to help them improve their fitness
C) Report them to the supervisor for poor performance
D) Make fun of them to motivate them to improve

27. The new team member seems embarrassed about their struggles. How do you support them?

A) Give them extra tasks to toughen them up
B) Provide encouragement and offer personal training tips
C) Ignore them and focus on your own training
D) Tell them they are not cut out for the job

28. During a particularly tough exercise, the new team member asks for a break. How do you respond?

A) Deny the break and push them harder
B) Allow a short break and offer to help them catch up
C) Tell them to quit if they can't handle it
D) Ignore their request and keep going

29. You notice the new team member is improving but still not at the required level. What do you do?

A) Continue offering support and encouragement
B) Report their slow progress to the supervisor
C) Stop helping and let them figure it out
D) Give them additional tasks to speed up their progress

30. The new team member has improved significantly. How do you acknowledge their progress?

A) Ignore their improvement
B) Compliment them privately
C) Publicly acknowledge their hard work
D) Give them more difficult tasks

Situation 7:

You are at the scene of a car accident with multiple injured people. The situation is chaotic, and the emergency response team is spread thin.

31. What should be your first action at the scene?

A) Start treating the first person you see
B) Assess the situation and prioritize the most critically injured
C) Wait for instructions from the team leader
D) Try to move everyone away from the accident site

32. You find a person with severe bleeding. What do you do first?

A) Call for medical backup
B) Apply pressure to stop the bleeding
C) Leave them to find the team leader
D) Check on other victims

33. A bystander is interfering with your work. How do you handle them?

A) Ignore them and focus on the victims
B) Politely ask them to step back and let you work
C) Yell at them to go away
D) Physically push them away

133

34. You need to evacuate a person from a car, but the door is jammed. What is your next step?

A) Leave them and find someone else to help
B) Use the appropriate tool to open the door
C) Break the window immediately
D) Wait for the team leader to arrive

35. A child is trapped in the back seat and is crying for help. What do you do?

A) Comfort them from outside the car
B) Focus on rescuing them immediately
C) Ignore them and help someone else
D) Call for specialized equipment

Situation 8:

You are conducting a fire safety inspection at a local business. You notice several safety violations that could pose serious risks.

36. What is your first course of action?

A) Ignore the violations and continue the inspection
B) Inform the business owner of the violations immediately
C) Shut down the business on the spot
D) Report the violations to your supervisor without informing the owner

37. The business owner is resistant to making changes. How do you handle this?

A) Ignore their resistance and leave
B) Explain the importance of the changes for safety
C) Threaten to shut down the business
D) Argue with them until they agree

38. You find a blocked emergency exit. What should you do?

A) Clear it yourself
B) Inform the owner and ensure it is cleared immediately
C) Ignore it and continue the inspection
D) Report it to your supervisor without taking action

39. During the inspection, you discover that the fire extinguishers are expired. What is your next step?

A) Ignore the expired extinguishers
B) Inform the owner and recommend immediate replacement
C) Remove the extinguishers

yourself
D) Report it to your supervisor and leave

40. The business owner agrees to address the violations. What should you do next?

A) Leave and trust they will follow through
B) Schedule a follow-up inspection to ensure compliance
C) Report their agreement to your supervisor
D) Ignore the follow-up and move on

Situation 9:

You are part of a team responding to a wildfire threatening a residential area. The wind is strong, and the fire is spreading quickly.

41. What should be your immediate priority?

A) Protecting the residential area
B) Fighting the fire at its source
C) Evacuating the residents
D) Waiting for further instructions

42. You are assigned to help evacuate residents. What is the first step?

A) Go door-to-door to alert residents
B) Use a loudspeaker to announce the evacuation
C) Start evacuating the closest houses
D) Call for additional evacuation support

43. A resident refuses to leave their home. How do you handle this?

A) Force them to leave
B) Respect their decision and move on
C) Explain the danger and strongly encourage them to leave
D) Call for law enforcement assistance

44. The fire is getting closer, and some residents are still packing their belongings. What do you do?

A) Help them pack to speed up the process
B) Urge them to leave immediately without packing
C) Leave them and focus on others
D) Wait until they are ready

45. After evacuating the residents, what should you do next?

A) Join the efforts to fight the fire
B) Take a break and rest
C) Check back on the evacuated area for stragglers
D) Wait for new instructions

Situation 10:

You are at the fire station, and an alarm goes off indicating a fire at a high-rise building. Your team prepares to respond immediately.

46. What is the first thing you should do before leaving the station?

A) Check all equipment is in working order
B) Call the building manager for details
C) Confirm the location and nature of the fire
D) Wait for the team leader's signal

47. Upon arrival, you see people trapped on upper floors. What is your immediate action?

A) Set up the ladder truck to reach them
B) Enter the building to assess the fire
C) Call for backup
D) Start evacuating the lower floors

48. Smoke is filling the stairwells, making evacuation difficult. What should you do?

A) Use the elevators
B) Guide people to safer areas within the building
C) Attempt to clear the smoke
D) Continue using the stairwells cautiously

49. A person on an upper floor signals for help. The ladder truck is already in use. What do you do?

A) Use a portable ladder to reach them
B) Wait for the ladder truck to become available
C) Enter the building to find another way to reach them
D) Tell them to wait until the ladder truck is free

50. After evacuating several people, you notice the fire spreading rapidly. What is your next move?

A) Focus on containing the fire
B) Continue evacuating people
C) Move to a safer location
D) Wait for further instructions

Situation 11:

You are part of a team conducting a training exercise in a simulated building collapse. One of your team members starts to panic and becomes unresponsive.

51. What is the first thing you should do?

A) Leave them and continue the exercise
B) Calm them down and try to get them to respond
C) Call for medical assistance
D) Report them to the supervisor

52. Your attempts to calm your team member are unsuccessful. What should you do next?

A) Continue without them
B) Escort them out of the simulation area
C) Call for backup to assist them
D) Leave them and focus on the task

53. Another team member offers to help. What is the best course of action?

A) Let them take over calming the panicked member
B) Both of you focus on calming them
C) Ask them to continue the exercise alone
D) Ignore their offer and proceed

54. The panicked team member becomes aggressive. How do you handle this?

A) Restrain them physically
B) Leave them alone
C) Call for professional help
D) Use calming techniques

55. The situation is resolved, and the panicked team member is safe. What should you do next?

A) Continue the exercise as planned
B) Report the incident to the supervisor
C) Take a break to debrief
D) End the exercise

Situation 12:

You are tasked with conducting a fire drill at a local school. The students and staff are unfamiliar with the procedures.

56. What is your first step in conducting the drill?

A) Conduct the drill without any prior notice
B) Explain the procedures to the staff and students beforehand
C) Wait for the school principal to give the go-ahead
D) Start the drill immediately

57. During the drill, some students are not taking it seriously. How do you handle this?

A) Ignore them and continue
B) Explain the importance of the drill and encourage participation
C) Punish them for not participating
D) Stop the drill

58. A teacher asks you to explain the best evacuation route. What do you do?

A) Give a brief explanation and move on
B) Show them the route and explain in detail
C) Tell them to follow the signs
D) Ignore the question

59. The alarm sounds, but some staff members are confused about their roles. What should you do?

A) Assign roles quickly and proceed with the drill
B) Stop the drill and clarify roles
C) Continue and address it later
D) Let them figure it out on their own

60. After the drill, what should be your next step?

A) Leave immediately
B) Conduct a debriefing session to discuss what went well and what needs improvement
C) Report to your supervisor and leave
D) Ignore the debriefing and move on

Situation 13:

You are at a public event providing fire safety information. A person approaches you with concerns about fire hazards in their apartment building.

61. What is your first response?

A) Give them a brochure and move on
B) Listen to their concerns and provide specific advice
C) Tell them to call the fire department
D) Ignore their concerns

62. The person mentions that the building manager is unresponsive. How do you proceed?

A) Advise them to contact local authorities
B) Offer to visit the building and assess the hazards
C) Suggest they move to a safer building
D) Tell them to keep trying to reach the manager

63. They ask if they can have a fire extinguisher in their apartment. What should you say?

A) It's not necessary
B) Recommend they get one and provide tips on how to use it
C) Tell them it's against regulations
D) Ignore the question

64. The person is also concerned about the lack of smoke detectors. What is your advice?

A) Install smoke detectors in their apartment
B) Ignore their concern
C) Tell them it's not important
D) Suggest they move to a different building

65. They thank you for your help. What should you do next?

A) Walk away
B) Offer additional resources and contact information
C) Ask them to leave
D) Ignore them and focus on others

Situation 14:

You are responding to a chemical spill in a warehouse. The area is hazardous, and there are reports of workers trapped inside.

66. What is your first action upon arrival?

A) Enter the warehouse immediately
B) Assess the situation and identify the chemicals involved
C) Wait for the hazardous materials team
D) Evacuate the surrounding area

67. You find a worker unconscious near the spill. What should you do?

A) Move them to a safe area
B) Leave them and find more help
C) Attempt to neutralize the spill
D) Call for medical assistance

68. The hazardous materials team arrives. What is your next step?

A) Take charge and direct the team
B) Assist the team by providing information about the situation
C) Leave the scene
D) Wait for their instructions

69. A worker is trapped in a contaminated area. How do you approach the rescue?

A) Enter the area without protective gear
B) Use appropriate protective equipment and follow protocols

C) Wait for the area to be cleared
D) Tell the worker to stay calm and wait for help

70. After the rescue, what is your next priority?

A) Go home and rest
B) Ensure all workers are accounted for and safe
C) Leave the cleanup to the hazardous materials team
D) Report the incident to your supervisor

Situation 15: You are part of a team conducting a fire safety presentation at a local community center. During the presentation, a fire alarm goes off.

71. What should you do first?

A) Continue with the presentation
B) Instruct everyone to evacuate calmly and orderly
C) Ignore the alarm and reassure everyone it's a drill
D) Panic and run out

72. Some people are panicking and not following the evacuation procedures. How do you handle this?

A) Yell at them to calm down
B) Guide them calmly and provide clear instructions
C) Leave them and focus on others
D) Call for security

73. You notice someone struggling to move quickly. What should you do?

A) Ignore them and keep moving
B) Assist them to the nearest exit
C) Ask someone else to help
D) Carry them out if necessary

74. After evacuating, some people want to re-enter the building. What is your response?

A) Allow them to re-enter
B) Prevent re-entry and explain the safety risks
C) Ignore them and let them decide
D) Call the fire department for guidance

75. The alarm turns out to be a false alarm. What should you do next?

A) Apologize and continue the presentation
B) Conduct a debriefing session about the evacuation
C) Leave the event
D) Ignore the false alarm and move on

Situation 16:

140

You are at the scene of a gas leak in a residential area. The smell of gas is strong, and residents are worried.

76. What is your first action?

A) Enter the building to locate the source
B) Evacuate residents from the area
C) Wait for the gas company to arrive
D) Ignore the smell and reassure residents

77. You find the source of the leak. What should you do next?

A) Attempt to fix it yourself
B) Evacuate the building and call for the gas company
C) Leave it and find the supervisor
D) Tell residents to stay indoors

79. A resident is refusing to evacuate. How do you handle this?

A) Force them to leave
B) Explain the danger and strongly encourage them to evacuate
C) Leave them and evacuate others
D) Ignore them

79. You notice a spark near the gas leak. What should be your immediate action?

A) Attempt to put out the spark
B) Evacuate immediately and warn others
C) Call for backup
D) Wait and watch

80. After the gas company fixes the leak, what should you do?

A) Allow residents to return immediately
B) Conduct a safety check before allowing re-entry
C) Leave without checking
D) Wait for the supervisor's instructions

Situation 17:

You are involved in a community outreach program to educate the public about fire prevention. During the session, a participant asks about the best way to prevent kitchen fires.

81. How should you respond?

A) Ignore the question and move on
B) Provide detailed information on kitchen fire prevention tips
C) Tell them to search online for answers
D) Change the subject to general fire safety

SPATIAL ORIENTATION PRACTICAL QUESTIONS

1: Which direction is North if you are facing East?

A) Right
B) Left
C) Behind
D) In front

2: If a car is traveling South, what direction is directly to its right?

A) East
B) West
C) North
D) South

3: You are facing West. Which direction do you turn to face South?

A) Left
B) Right
C) Behind
D) In front

4: If you walk 10 steps East and then 5 steps South, which direction must you walk to return to your starting point?

A) West, then North
B) North, then West
C) South, then East
D) East, then North

5: Which direction is to your left if you are facing North?

A) West
B) East
C) South
D) North

6: A train is moving North. Which direction is to its left?

A) West
B) East
C) South
D) North

7: If you are facing South and turn 90 degrees to your right, which direction are you facing?

A) West
B) East
C) North
D) South

8: You walk 10 steps North and then 10 steps West. Which direction do you need to go to return to your starting point?

A) South, then East
B) East, then South
C) North, then West
D) West, then South

9: If you are traveling West, which direction is directly behind you?

A) East
B) North
C) South
D) West

10: Which direction is to your right if you are facing West?

A) North
B) South
C) East
D) West

11: You turn left from facing North. Which direction are you now facing?

A) West
B) East
C) South
D) North

12: If you walk 5 steps East and then 5 steps North, which direction do you need to go to return to your starting point?

A) West, then South
B) South, then West
C) North, then East
D) East, then North

13: A bus is traveling East. Which direction is to its right?

A) South
B) North
C) West
D) East

14: If you are facing East and turn 180 degrees, which direction are you now facing?

A) West
B) North
C) South
D) East

15: You walk 7 steps South and then 3 steps East. Which direction do you need to go to return to your starting point?

A) North, then West
B) West, then North
C) South, then East
D) East, then North

16: Which direction is to your right if you are facing South?

A) West
B) East
C) North
D) South

17: If you turn right from facing West, which direction are you now facing?

A) North
B) South
C) East
D) West

18: A cyclist is traveling North. Which direction is directly behind them?

A) South
B) West
C) East
D) North

19: If you walk 8 steps North and then 4 steps West, which direction do you need to go to return to your starting point?

A) South, then East
B) East, then South
C) North, then West
D) West, then South

20: Which direction is to your left if you are facing East?

A) North
B) South
C) West
D) East

21: You turn left from facing South. Which direction are you now facing?

A) East
B) West
C) North
D) South

22: If you are traveling North, which direction is directly to your right?

A) East
B) West
C) South
D) North

23: You walk 6 steps East and then 9 steps North. Which direction do you need to go to return to your starting point?

A) West, then South
B) South, then West
C) North, then East
D) East, then North

24: If you are facing West and turn 90 degrees to your left, which direction are you now facing?

A) South
B) East
C) North
D) West

144

25: Which direction is to your right if you are facing North?

A) East
B) West
C) South
D) North

26: You turn right from facing East. Which direction are you now facing?

A) South
B) West
C) North
D) East

27: If you are traveling South, which direction is directly behind you?

A) North
B) East
C) West
D) South

28: You walk 10 steps West and then 5 steps South. Which direction do you need to go to return to your starting point?

A) North, then East
B) East, then North
C) South, then West
D) West, then North

29: If you are facing South and turn 180 degrees, which direction are you now facing?

A) North
B) West
C) East
D) South

30: Which direction is to your left if you are facing South?

A) East
B) West
C) North
D) South

31: You turn left from facing East. Which direction are you now facing?

A) North
B) South
C) West
D) East

32: If you walk 4 steps North and then 8 steps East, which direction do you need to go to return to your starting point?

A) West, then South
B) South, then West
C) North, then East
D) East, then North

33: Which direction is directly behind you if you are facing East?

A) West
B) North
C) South
D) East

34: You are traveling North and turn 90 degrees to your left. Which direction are you now facing?

A) West
B) East
C) South
D) North

35: Which direction is to your right if you are facing East?

A) South
B) North
C) West
D) East

36: If you walk 6 steps South and then 2 steps West, which direction do you need to go to return to your starting point?

A) North, then East
B) East, then North
C) South, then West
D) West, then North

37: You turn right from facing South. Which direction are you now facing?

A) West
B) East
C) North
D) South

38: Which direction is directly behind you if you are traveling East?

A) West
B) North
C) South
D) East

39: You walk 3 steps West and then 7 steps North. Which direction do you need to go to return to your starting point?

A) South, then East
B) East, then South
C) North, then West
D) West, then South

40: If you are facing North and turn 90 degrees to your right, which direction are you now facing?

A) East
B) West
C) South
D) North

41: Which direction is to your left if you are facing West?

A) South
B) North
C) East
D) West

42: You turn left from facing West. Which direction are you now facing?

A) South
B) East
C) North
D) West

43: If you walk 5 steps South and then 5 steps East, which direction do you need to go to return to your starting point?

A) North, then West
B) West, then North
C) South, then East
D) East, then North

44: Which direction is directly behind you if you are facing North?

A) South
B) East
C) West
D) North

45: You are traveling South and turn 90 degrees to your left. Which direction are you now facing?

A) East
B) West
C) North
D) South

46: Which direction is to your right if you are facing South?

A) West
B) East
C) North
D) South

47: If you walk 8 steps North and then 6 steps East, which direction do you need to go to return to your starting point?

A) South, then West
B) West, then South
C) North, then East
D) East, then North

48: You turn right from facing North. Which direction are you now facing?

A) East
B) West
C) South
D) North

49: Which direction is directly behind you if you are traveling West?

A) East
B) North
C) South
D) West

50: You walk 7 steps East and then 4 steps North. Which direction do you need to go to return to your starting point?

A) South, then West
B) West, then South
C) North, then East
D) East, then North

51: If you are facing West and turn 180 degrees, which direction are you now facing?

A) East
B) North
C) South
D) West

52: Which direction is to your left if you are facing East?

A) North
B) South
C) West
D) East

53: You turn left from facing North. Which direction are you now facing?

A) West
B) East
C) South
D) North

54: If you walk 9 steps South and then 3 steps East, which direction do you need to go to return to your starting point?

A) North, then West
B) West, then North
C) South, then East
D) East, then North

55: Which direction is directly behind you if you are facing South?

A) North
B) East
C) West
D) South

56: You are traveling East and turn 90 degrees to your right. Which direction are you now facing?

A) South
B) North
C) West
D) East

57: Which direction is to your right if you are facing West?

A) North
B) South
C) East
D) West

58: If you walk 4 steps North and then 5 steps East, which direction do you need to go to return to your starting point?

A) South, then West
B) West, then South
C) North, then East
D) East, then North

59: You turn right from facing East. Which direction are you now facing?

A) South
B) West
C) North
D) East

60: Which direction is directly behind you if you are traveling North?

A) South
B) East
C) West
D) North

61: You walk 10 steps South and then 8 steps East. Which direction do you need to go to return to your starting point?

A) North, then West
B) West, then North
C) South, then East
D) East, then North

62: If you are facing South and turn 90 degrees to your left, which direction are you now facing?

A) East
B) West
C) North
D) South

63: Which direction is to your left if you are facing North?

A) West
B) East
C) South
D) North

64: You turn left from facing South. Which direction are you now facing?

A) East
B) West
C) North
D) South

65: If you walk 3 steps North and then 7 steps East, which direction do you need to go to return to your starting point?

A) South, then West
B) West, then South
C) North, then East
D) East, then North

66: Which direction is directly behind you if you are facing West?

A) East
B) North
C) South
D) West

67: You are traveling East and turn 90 degrees to your left. Which direction are you now facing?

A) North
B) South
C) West
D) East

68: Which direction is to your right if you are facing East?

A) South
B) North
C) West
D) East

69: If you walk 5 steps South and then 8 steps West, which direction do you need to go to return to your starting point?

A) North, then East
B) East, then North
C) South, then West
D) West, then North

70: You turn right from facing North. Which direction are you now facing?

A) East
B) West
C) South
D) North

71: Which direction is directly behind you if you are traveling South?

A) North
B) East
C) West
D) South

72: You walk 2 steps East and then 6 steps South. Which direction do you need to go to return to your starting point?

A) West, then North
B) North, then West
C) South, then East
D) East, then North

73: If you are facing East and turn 90 degrees to your left, which direction are you now facing?

A) North
B) South
C) West
D) East

74: Which direction is to your left if you are facing South?

A) East
B) West
C) North
D) South

75: You turn left from facing West. Which direction are you now facing?

A) South
B) East
C) North
D) West

76: If you walk 6 steps North and then 9 steps East, which direction do you need to go to return to your starting point?

A) West, then South
B) South, then West
C) North, then East
D) East, then North

77: Which direction is directly behind you if you are facing East?

A) West
B) North
C) South
D) East

78: You are traveling South and turn 90 degrees to your right. Which direction are you now facing?

A) West
B) East
C) North
D) South

79: Which direction is to your right if you are facing North?

A) East
B) West
C) South
D) North

80: If you walk 7 steps South and then 4 steps East, which direction do you need to go to return to your starting point?

A) North, then West
B) West, then North
C) South, then East
D) East, then North

81: You turn right from facing South. Which direction are you now facing?

A) West
B) East
C) North
D) South

READING COMPREHENSION ANSWER KEY

1. **C) Its flexible spine**

   Explanation: The passage mentions that the cheetah's incredible speed is due to its long, powerful legs, large nasal passages, and a flexible spine. The flexible spine specifically allows it to extend its body further with each stride.

2. **B) 500 meters**

   Explanation: The passage states that cheetahs can cover distances up to 500 meters in short bursts.

3. **D) 60 miles per hour**

   Explanation: The passage indicates that cheetahs can reach speeds up to 60 miles per hour.

4. **D) Long, powerful legs**

   Explanation: The passage attributes the cheetah's speed to its long, powerful legs, large nasal passages, and flexible spine.

5. **A) They tire quickly**

   Explanation: The passage implies that cheetahs can only maintain their top speed for short distances, suggesting that they tire quickly.

6. **B) Photovoltaic cells**

   Explanation: The passage explains that solar panels convert sunlight into electricity using photovoltaic cells.

7. **B) On sunny days**

   Explanation: The passage states that solar panels work best on sunny days.

8. **C) Proper installation**

   Explanation: Proper installation, including the optimal angle and direction, can significantly improve the efficiency of solar panels.

9. **A) Yes**

Explanation: The passage mentions that solar panels can still generate some power on cloudy days.

10. **C) The angle and direction**

Explanation: Proper installation, which includes the optimal angle and direction, is important for the efficiency of solar panels.

11. **B) They help in pollination**

Explanation: The passage highlights the critical role of honeybees in pollination, which is essential for the reproduction of many plants.

12. **C) Nectar and pollen**

Explanation: Honeybees collect nectar and pollen to produce honey.

13. **B) For the reproduction of plants**

Explanation: The passage states that pollination is essential for the reproduction of many plants.

14. **B) By producing honey**

Explanation: Honeybees benefit humans by producing honey and aiding in crop production through pollination.

15. **B) Nectar**

Explanation: The main food source for honeybees is nectar.

16. **B) Being the highest mountain**

Explanation: The passage identifies Mount Everest as the highest mountain in the world.

17. **B) 29,032 feet**

Explanation: The passage states that Mount Everest stands at 29,032 feet above sea level.

18. **C) Altitude sickness**

Explanation: The passage lists extreme weather, altitude sickness, and difficult terrain as challenges climbers face on Mount Everest.

19. **C) To conquer the highest peak**

Explanation: The passage explains that climbers from all over the globe are attracted to Mount Everest to conquer the highest peak.

20. **B) Extreme weather**

Explanation: Besides its height, extreme weather makes Mount Everest challenging.

21. **C) Chlorophyll**

Explanation: The passage mentions that plants use chlorophyll to carry out photosynthesis.

22. **B) Glucose and oxygen**

Explanation: The passage states that photosynthesis converts carbon dioxide and water into glucose and oxygen.

23. **B) It provides energy for the process**

Explanation: Sunlight provides the energy needed for the process of photosynthesis.

24. **B) It synthesizes foods for growth**

Explanation: Photosynthesis is important for plants because it synthesizes foods that provide the energy necessary for growth.

25. **C) Carbon dioxide**

Explanation: The passage mentions that carbon dioxide is one of the inputs required for photosynthesis.

26. **C) To protect against invasions**

Explanation: The Great Wall of China was originally built to protect Chinese states from invasions.

27. **C) 13,000 miles**

Explanation: The passage states that the Great Wall of China stretches over 13,000 miles.

28. **C) Historical strength and perseverance**

Explanation: Today, the Great Wall stands as a testament to China's historical strength and perseverance.

29. **C) A wall**

Explanation: The passage describes the Great Wall as a wall.

30. **B) Ancient China**

Explanation: The Great Wall primarily represents Ancient China, particularly the period when it was built.

31. **C) Johannes Gutenberg**

Explanation: The passage identifies Johannes Gutenberg as the inventor of the printing press.

32. **B) 15th century**

Explanation: The printing press was invented in the 15th century.

33. **C) Improved accessibility to books**

Explanation: The passage explains that the printing press made books more accessible and reduced costs.

34. **C) It increased them**

Explanation: The passage states that the printing press contributed to the rise in literacy rates across Europe.

35. **B) Information became more accessible**

Explanation: The printing press made information more accessible, which revolutionized the spread of information.

36. **C) Bacterial infections**

Explanation: The passage states that antibiotics combat bacterial infections.

37. **C) Early 20th century**

Explanation: Antibiotics were developed in the early 20th century.

38. **B) Tuberculosis**

Explanation: The passage mentions that antibiotics have helped treat diseases such as tuberculosis and pneumonia.

39. **B) Revolutionized the treatment of diseases**

Explanation: The development of antibiotics revolutionized the treatment of bacterial infections.

40. **A) They have saved countless lives**

Explanation: The passage states that antibiotics have saved countless lives and revolutionized the treatment of diseases.

41. **C) Leonardo da Vinci**

Explanation: The passage identifies Leonardo da Vinci as the painter of the Mona Lisa.

42. **B) The Louvre Museum**

Explanation: The Mona Lisa is displayed at the Louvre Museum in Paris.

43. **C) Its enigmatic expression**

Explanation: The passage notes that the Mona Lisa is known for its enigmatic expression.

44. **C) Millions**

Explanation: The passage mentions that the Mona Lisa attracts millions of visitors each year.

45. **C) Paris**

Explanation: The Louvre Museum, where the Mona Lisa is displayed, is located in Paris.

46. **A) The Wright brothers**

Explanation: The passage states that the Wright brothers invented the airplane.

47. **B) 1903**

Explanation: The Wright brothers achieved their first successful flight in 1903.

48. **B) Kitty Hawk**

Explanation: The Wright brothers' first successful flight took place at Kitty Hawk.

49. **B) The feasibility of controlled, sustained flight**

Explanation: The passage explains that the Wright brothers' invention demonstrated the feasibility of controlled, sustained flight.

50. **C) Aviation**

Explanation: The Wright brothers' invention paved the way for the future of aviation.

51. **B) Radioactivity**

Explanation: The passage states that Marie Curie researched radioactivity.

52. **B) Two**

Explanation: Marie Curie won two Nobel Prizes.

53. **B) Physics and Chemistry**

Explanation: Marie Curie won Nobel Prizes in Physics and Chemistry.

54. **C) X-ray machines**

Explanation: The passage mentions that Curie's discoveries laid the groundwork for the development of X-ray machines.

55. **B) They advanced the field of science**

Explanation: Marie Curie's discoveries advanced the field of science.

56. **D) Neil Armstrong**

Explanation: The passage identifies Neil Armstrong as the first person to walk on the moon.

57. **C) 1969**

Explanation: Neil Armstrong walked on the moon on July 20, 1969.

58. **C) "That's one small step for man, one giant leap for mankind"**

Explanation: The passage quotes Neil Armstrong's famous words when he stepped on the moon.

59. **B) Human achievement in space exploration**

Explanation: Neil Armstrong's moonwalk symbolizes human achievement in space exploration.

60. **B) American**

Explanation: The passage states that Neil Armstrong was an American astronaut.

61. **B) William Shakespeare**

Explanation: The passage identifies William Shakespeare as one of the greatest playwrights in history.

62. **C) "Hamlet"**

Explanation: "Hamlet" is one of the works authored by Shakespeare.

63. **B) Intricate plots**

Explanation: Shakespeare's works are known for their intricate plots, rich characters, and profound themes.

64. **B) "Macbeth"**

Explanation: "Macbeth" is one of the plays written by Shakespeare.

65. **B) Profound themes about human nature**

Explanation: Shakespeare's works often explore profound themes about human nature.

66. **B) Alexander Fleming**

Explanation: The passage states that Alexander Fleming discovered penicillin.

67. **B) 1928**

Explanation: Penicillin was discovered in 1928.

68. **C) Bacterial infections**

Explanation: The passage mentions that penicillin revolutionized the treatment of bacterial infections.

69. **B) It revolutionized the treatment of bacterial infections** Explanation: The discovery of penicillin revolutionized the treatment of bacterial infections.

70. **B) The development of other antibiotics**

Explanation: The discovery of penicillin led to the development of numerous other antibiotics.

71. **B) Shah Jahan**

Explanation: The passage states that the Taj Mahal was built by Emperor Shah Jahan.

72. **C) In memory of Shah Jahan's wife**

Explanation: The Taj Mahal was built in memory of Shah Jahan's wife, Mumtaz Mahal.

73. **D) Agra** Explanation: The Taj Mahal is located in Agra, India.

74. **C) White marble** Explanation: The passage describes the Taj Mahal as being made primarily of white marble.

75. **C) Its intricate artistry and harmonious proportions** Explanation: The Taj Mahal is renowned for its intricate artistry and harmonious proportions.

76. **C) Colorado River**

    Explanation: The passage states that the Grand Canyon was carved by the Colorado River.

77. **B) Geological history**

    Explanation: The passage mentions that the Grand Canyon reveals millions of years of geological history.

78. **B) Arizona**

    Explanation: The Grand Canyon is located in Arizona.

79. **C) To view its vast and colorful landscape**

    Explanation: Millions of tourists visit the Grand Canyon each year to view its vast and colorful landscape.

80. **C) Its geological formations**

    Explanation: The Grand Canyon is famous for its geological formations.

81. **B) 1990**

    Explanation: The passage states that the Hubble Space Telescope was launched in 1990.

MATHEMATICAL REASONING ANSWER KEY

1. **C) 6**

   Explanation: According to the order of operations, $2+2\times3=2+6=8$.

2. **C) 6**

   Explanation: $5x-3=2x+12 \Rightarrow 3x=15 \Rightarrow x=5$.

3. **A) 40**

   Explanation: Average speed is $\frac{60 \text{ miles}}{1.5 \text{ hours}}=40$ mph.

4. **B) $\frac{3}{5}$**

   Explanation: Simplifying $\frac{15}{25}$ by dividing both the numerator and the denominator by 5 gives $\frac{3}{5}$.

5. **A) 15 square units**

   Explanation: Area of a rectangle is length $\times$ width$=5\times3=15$.

6. **D) 13**

   Explanation: $2x^2-4x+1=2(3)^2-4(3)+1=18-12+1=7$.

7. **B) 6**

   Explanation: $2x+5=17 \Rightarrow 2x=12 \Rightarrow x=6$.

8. **B) 180**

   Explanation: The sum of the interior angles of a triangle is always 180 degrees.

9. **C) 3**

   Explanation: $3y-2=7 \Rightarrow 3y=9 \Rightarrow y=3$.

10. **A) 16**

    Explanation: $5^2-3^2=25-9=16$.

11. **B) 25.12 units**

    Explanation: Circumference of a circle is $2\pi r \approx 2\times3.14\times4=25.12$.

12. **C) 15**

    Explanation: $\frac{3}{4}$ of 20 is $\frac{3}{4}\times20=15$.

13. **A) 30**

    Explanation: Miles per gallon is $\frac{150 \text{ miles}}{5 \text{ gallons}}=30$ mpg.

14. **B) $6x^2$**

    Explanation: $2x \times 3x = \mathbf{6x^2}$.

15. **B) 7**

    Explanation: $\sqrt{49} = 7$.

16. **C) 10**

    Explanation: $3a - b = 3(4) - 2 = 12 - 2 = 10$.

17. **B) 3**

    Explanation: $4z + 6 = 18 \Rightarrow 4z = 12 \Rightarrow z = 3$.

18. **B) 20**

    Explanation: 10%10\%10% of 200 is $0.1 \times 200 = 20$.

19. **B) 8**

    Explanation: Perimeter $= 2 \times$ (length + width) $= 24 \Rightarrow 2 \times (6 + x) = 24 \Rightarrow x = 8$.

20. **A) $\frac{2}{3}$**

    Explanation: Simplifying $\frac{24}{36}$ by dividing both the numerator and the denominator by 12 gives $\frac{2}{3}$.

21. **C) 5**

    Explanation: $7x - 5 = 16 \Rightarrow 7x = 21 \Rightarrow x = 3$.

22. **C) 64**

    Explanation: $8^2 = 64$.

23. **A) 12 square units**

    Explanation: Area of a triangle is $\frac{1}{2} \times \text{base} \times \text{height} = \frac{1}{2} \times 6 \times 4 = 12$.

24. **A) $\frac{3}{4}$.**

    Explanation: Converting 0.75 to a fraction gives $\frac{3}{4}$.

25. **B) 4**

    Explanation: $2y + 4 = 12 \Rightarrow 2y = 8 \Rightarrow y = 4$.

26. **C) 64**

    Explanation: $4^3 = 4 \times 4 \times 4 = 64$.

27. **B) $\frac{3}{2}$.**

    Explanation: Simplifying $\frac{18}{24}$ by dividing both the numerator and the denominator by 6 gives $\frac{3}{2}$.

28. **D) 0**

    Explanation: $x^3 - 3x = 2^3 - 3(2) = 8 - 6 = 2$.

29. **B) 5**

    Explanation: $3x + 4 = 19 \Rightarrow 3x = 15 \Rightarrow x = 5$.

30. **C) 20 units**

Explanation: Perimeter of a square is 4×side length=4×5=20

31. **B) $\frac{1}{4}$**

Explanation: Converting 25% to a fraction gives $\frac{1}{4}$.

32. **B) 81**

Explanation: 9^2=81.

33. **C) 5 units**

Explanation: The radius is half of the diameter, so $\frac{10}{2}$=5.

34. **C) 5**

Explanation: 5y−2=3y+8 ⟹ 2y=10 ⟹ y=5.

35. **C) 9**

Explanation: $\sqrt{81}$=9.

36. **A) $\frac{2}{3}$**

Explanation: Simplifying $\frac{28}{42}$ by dividing both the numerator and the denominator by 14 gives $\frac{2}{3}$.

37. **A) 153.86 square units**

Explanation: Area of a circle is πr^2≈3.14×7^2=153.86.

38. **B) 4**

Explanation: 6z+9=33 ⟹ 6z=24 ⟹ z=4.

39. **B) 6**

Explanation: 12×12=6.

40. **D) Right**

Explanation: A triangle with sides 3, 4, and 5 units is a right triangle because $3^2+4^2=5^2$.

41. **D) 4**

Explanation: 4x−7=9 ⟹ 4x=16 ⟹ x=4.

42. **C) 27 cubic units**

Explanation: Volume of a cube is side length^3=3^3=27.

43. **A) 35**

Explanation: Converting 0.6 to a fraction gives 35.

44. **B) 53**

Explanation: 7^2+2^2=49+4=53.

45. **D) 6**

Explanation: 4y−5=11 ⟹ 4y=16 ⟹ y=4.

46. **D) $\frac{3}{5}$**

Explanation: Simplifying $\frac{45}{60}$ by dividing both the numerator and the denominator by 15 gives $\frac{3}{5}$.

47. **A) 6**

Explanation: $x^2-4x+3=5^2-4(5)+3=25-20+3=8$.

48. **C) 5**

Explanation: $5z+10=35 \Rightarrow 5z=25 \Rightarrow z=5$.

49. **B) 30**

Explanation: 20% of 150 is $0.2 \times 150=30$.

50. **B) 25.12 units**

Explanation: Circumference of a circle is $\pi d \approx 3.14 \times 8=25.12$.

51. **D) 4**

Explanation: $2x+7=15 \Rightarrow 2x=8 \Rightarrow x=4$.

52. **B) 36**

Explanation: $6^2=36$.

53. **C) $\frac{4}{5}$**

Explanation: Simplifying $\frac{32}{40}$ by dividing both the numerator and the denominator by 8 gives $\frac{4}{5}$.

54. **D) $\frac{1}{5}$**

Explanation: Converting 0.2 to a fraction gives $\frac{1}{5}$.

55. **C) 32 square units**

Explanation: Area of a rectangle is length× width $=8 \times 4=32$.

56. **B) 5**

Explanation: $3y+6=21 \Rightarrow 3y=15 \Rightarrow y=5$.

57. **B) 50**

Explanation: $10^2-5^2=100-25=50$.

58. **B) 24 cubic units**

Explanation: Volume of a rectangular prism is length× width ×height$=4 \times 3 \times 2=24$.

59. **A) $\frac{1}{2}$**

Explanation: Converting 50% to a fraction gives $\frac{1}{2}$.

60. **C) 27**

Explanation: 3^2=27.

61. **A) $\frac{2}{3}$**

Explanation: Simplifying $\frac{14}{21}$ by dividing both the numerator and the denominator by 7 gives $\frac{2}{3}$.

62. **A) 20 square units**

Explanation: Area of a triangle is
12×base×height=12×8×5=20.

63. **C) 4**

Explanation: 9x−4=32 ⟹ 9x=36 ⟹ x=4.

64. **C) 8**

Explanation: $\sqrt{64}$=8.

65. **A) 19**

Explanation: 2a+3b=2(3)+3(5) =6+15=21.

66. **D) 125**

Explanation: 53=5×5×5=125.

67. **A) 4**

Explanation: 8z+12=52 ⟹ 8z=40 ⟹ z=5.

68. **B) 20**

Explanation: 25% of 80 is 0.25×80=20.

69. **C) 32 units**

Explanation: Perimeter of a rectangle is 2×(length+width) =2× (10+6) =32.

70. **D) 12**

Explanation: Converting 0.5 to a fraction gives 12.

71. **C) 16**

Explanation: 2^4=16.

72. **A) $\frac{2}{3}$**

Explanation: Simplifying $\frac{48}{60}$ by dividing both the numerator and the denominator by 12 gives $\frac{2}{3}$

73. **D) 5**

Explanation: 7y+2=23 ⟹ 7y=21 ⟹ y=5.

74. **C) 6**

Explanation: $\sqrt{36}$=6.

75. **A) 141.3 cubic units**

Explanation: Volume of a cylinder is $\pi r^2 h \approx 3.14 \times 3^2 \times 5 = 141.3$.

76. **A) 36 square units**

Explanation: Area of a square is side $\text{length}^2 = 6^2 = 36$.

77. **D) $\frac{2}{5}$**

Explanation: Converting 0.4 to a fraction gives $\frac{2}{5}$.

78. **C) 8**

Explanation: $3x+4=25 \Rightarrow 3x=21 \Rightarrow x=7$

79. **A) 64**

Explanation: $8^2=64$.

80. **B) $\frac{3}{4}$**

Explanation: Simplifying $\frac{21}{28}$ by dividing both the numerator and the denominator by 7 gives $\frac{3}{4}$.

81. **C) 30**

Explanation: 15% of 200 is $0.15 \times 200 = 30$.

MECHANICAL REASONING ANSWER KEY

1. **A) Caliper**

   Explanation: A caliper is used to measure the internal diameter of a pipe accurately.

2. **A) First class**

   Explanation: A seesaw is a first-class lever where the fulcrum is between the load and the effort.

3. **B) Reduces effort**

   Explanation: The main advantage of a pulley system is that it reduces the effort needed to lift a load.

4. **C) Motor**

   Explanation: A motor converts electrical energy into mechanical energy.

5. **C) Spur gear**

   Explanation: Spur gears have teeth that are straight and parallel to the axis.

6. **B) To store energy**

   Explanation: A flywheel stores rotational energy to keep the engine running smoothly.

7. **A) Increases distance**

   Explanation: An inclined plane reduces the effort needed to lift a load by increasing the distance over which the force is applied.

8. **B) 5**

   Explanation: The mechanical advantage of a lever is the ratio of the effort arm to the load arm, which is 5/1=5.

9. **B) Bearing**

   Explanation: Bearings reduce friction between moving parts in a car.

10. **C) Oil**

    Explanation: A hydraulic system uses oil to transmit force.

11. **A) Between the load and effort**

    Explanation: In a first-class lever, the fulcrum is located between the load and the effort.

12. **B) To allow rotation in one direction only**

Explanation: A ratchet mechanism allows rotation in one direction only, preventing backward movement.

13. **B) Pulley**

Explanation: A pulley is a simple machine consisting of a wheel with a rope or belt around it.

14. **A) By using threads**

Explanation: A screw converts rotational motion into linear motion through its threads.

15. **B) Potential**

Explanation: A compressed spring stores potential energy.

16. **B) Regulates the timing of the valves** Explanation: A camshaft regulates the timing of the valves in an engine.

17. **B) By meshing gears with different orientations**

Explanation: A gear train changes the direction of force by meshing gears with different orientations.

18. **C) Bevel gear**

Explanation: Bevel gears are used to transmit motion between intersecting shafts.

19. **C) Pascal's law**

Explanation: A hydraulic press operates based on Pascal's law, which states that pressure applied to a confined fluid is transmitted equally in all directions.

20. **B) Single movable pulley**

Explanation: A single movable pulley reduces the effort needed to lift a load by half.

21. **C) By separating objects**

Explanation: A wedge works by separating objects.

22. **B) To convert linear motion to rotational motion**

Explanation: A crankshaft converts linear motion to rotational motion in an engine.

23. **B) Crankshaft**

Explanation: A crankshaft converts linear motion into rotational motion.

24. **B) Camshaft**

Explanation: A camshaft controls the intake and exhaust of the air-fuel mixture in an engine.

25. **B) By allowing wheels to rotate at different speeds**
Explanation: A differential gear allows wheels to rotate at different speeds, especially when turning.

26. **A) To convert mechanical energy into electrical energy** Explanation: An alternator converts mechanical energy into electrical energy in a vehicle.

27. **C) Linear**

Explanation: A piston in an engine performs linear motion.

28. **C) Torque wrench**

Explanation: A torque wrench is used to tighten or loosen bolts with a specific torque.

29. **C) Rotational speed of an engine**

Explanation: A tachometer measures the rotational speed of an engine.

30. **C) By using centrifugal force**

Explanation: A centrifugal pump moves fluid by using centrifugal force.

31. **C) To prevent leakage**

Explanation: A gasket in an engine prevents leakage.

32. **B) By regulating temperature**

Explanation: A thermostat in a car engine regulates temperature.

33. **B) To cool the engine**

Explanation: A radiator cools the engine in a vehicle.

34. **A) Transmits power between pulleys**

Explanation: A belt drive transmits power between pulleys.

35. **B) By using hydraulic pressure**

Explanation: A hydraulic jack lifts heavy loads by using hydraulic pressure.

36.   **D) Ball bearing**

Explanation: Ball bearings reduce friction between a rotating shaft and a fixed housing.

37.   **C) To protect against overcurrent**

Explanation: A fuse protects an electrical circuit against overcurrent.

38.   **B) By using rotating cups**

Explanation: An anemometer measures wind speed by using rotating cups.

39.   **B) Voltage**

Explanation: A voltmeter measures voltage.

40.   **B) By using induction**

Explanation: A transformer changes voltage levels by using induction.

41.   **D) Principle of moments**

Explanation: The principle of operation for a lever is the principle of moments.

42.   **B) Second class**

Explanation: A wheelbarrow is a second-class lever where the load is between the fulcrum and the effort.

43.   **C) By increasing effort arm**

Explanation: Mechanical advantage increases with a lever by increasing the effort arm.

44.   **B) To regulate the motion of a follower**

Explanation: A cam regulates the motion of a follower in mechanical systems.

45.   **C) Higher ratio decreases speed**

Explanation: In a gear train, a higher gear ratio decreases speed.

46.   **B) To engage and disengage power transmission**

Explanation: A clutch engages and disengages power transmission in a vehicle.

170

47. **D) By measuring fluid pressure**

Explanation: A pressure gauge works by measuring fluid pressure.

48. **C) Oscillating**

Explanation: A pendulum exhibits oscillating motion.

49. **B) To control the flow of fluid**

Explanation: A valve in a hydraulic system controls the flow of fluid.

50. **D) It has a screw-like thread**

Explanation: A worm gear has a screw-like thread.

51. **B) To seal the combustion chamber**

Explanation: A piston ring seals the combustion chamber in an engine.

52. **A) By using mercury**

Explanation: A barometer measures atmospheric pressure by using mercury.

53. **B) To control a high-power circuit with a low-power signal** Explanation: A relay controls a high-power circuit with a low-power signal.

54. **B) By meshing gears of different sizes**

Explanation: A simple gear train works by meshing gears of different sizes.

55. **B) Rotational**

Explanation: A crank handle provides rotational motion.

56. **B) To remove impurities from the air**

Explanation: An air filter in an engine removes impurities from the air.

57. **C) By using centrifugal force**

Explanation: A centrifugal clutch works by using centrifugal force.

58. **B) To transmit torque from the engine to the wheels** Explanation: A drive shaft transmits torque from the engine to the wheels in a vehicle.

59. **B) By using the Earth's magnetic field**

Explanation: A magnetic compass works by using the Earth's magnetic field.

60. **C) Linear bearing**

Explanation: A linear bearing allows linear motion.

61. **C) Pascal's law**

Explanation: A hydraulic lift operates based on Pascal's law.

62. **B) By converting kinetic energy to heat**

Explanation: A brake system in a car works by converting kinetic energy to heat.

63. **A) To store rotational energy**

Explanation: A flywheel stores rotational energy in a mechanical system.

64. **B) By using compressed air**

Explanation: A pneumatic system transmits power by using compressed air.

65. **C) To change speed and torque**

Explanation: A gearbox changes speed and torque.

66. **C) By transmitting motion between intersecting shafts** Explanation: A bevel gear transmits motion between intersecting shafts.

67. **C) To transmit and multiply torque**

Explanation: A torque converter transmits and multiplies torque in a vehicle.

68. **C) By using a diaphragm that moves back and forth** Explanation: A diaphragm pump operates by using a diaphragm that moves back and forth.

69. **C) To protect against overcurrent**

Explanation: A fuse in an electrical circuit protects against overcurrent.

70. **B) By using hydraulic fluid to exert force**

Explanation: A hydraulic press works by using hydraulic fluid to exert force.

71. **D) Electrical**

Explanation: A capacitor stores electrical energy.

72. **C) By using friction between surfaces**

Explanation: A friction clutch works by using friction between surfaces.

73. **B) To regulate the timing of the valves**

Explanation: A camshaft regulates the timing of the valves in an engine.

74. **D) By using a screw-like thread**

Explanation: A worm gear works by using a screw-like thread.

75. **C) To prevent leakage**

Explanation: A gasket in an engine prevents leakage.

76. **C) By counting rotations per minute**

Explanation: A tachometer measures rotational speed by counting rotations per minute.

77. **C) Linear**

Explanation: A piston in an engine performs linear motion.

78. **A) To convert mechanical energy into electrical energy** Explanation: An alternator converts mechanical energy into electrical energy in a vehicle.

79. **C) By using a diaphragm that moves back and forth** Explanation: A diaphragm pump operates by using a diaphragm that moves back and forth.

80. **C) To change speed and torque**

Explanation: A gearbox changes speed and torque.

81. **B) By using compressed air**

Explanation: A pneumatic system transmits power by using compressed air.

SITUATIONAL JUDGMENT ANSWER KEY

1. **C) Perform a risk assessment and plan a rescue operation**

   Explanation: Conducting a risk assessment and planning ensures the safety of both the rescuers and the victims, enabling an effective and coordinated rescue effort.

2. **D) Ensure the safety of your team and the surrounding area**

   Explanation: Safety of the team and ensuring the area is secured is crucial to prevent further casualties and to prepare for a safe rescue operation.

3. **C) Calmly explain the danger and assure her you are handling the situation**

   Explanation: Calming the woman and ensuring her cooperation prevents her from endangering herself or others while allowing you to focus on the rescue.

4. **B) Carry the child outside to safety**

   Explanation: Removing the child from the immediate danger and ensuring they receive medical attention is the priority.

5. **B) Inform your team and evacuate the area**

   Explanation: The presence of a propane tank is a significant risk, and informing the team ensures they are aware of the danger and can take appropriate action to avoid an explosion.

6. **A) Confront your colleague directly and ask them to follow the protocols**

   Explanation: Addressing the issue directly with your colleague allows them an opportunity to correct their behavior before escalating the matter.

7. **C) Document their behavior and report it to your supervisor**

   Explanation: Documenting and reporting the behavior ensures that there is a record and that the issue is handled by someone with authority to enforce safety protocols.

8. **C) Talk to the supervisor privately after the meeting**

   Explanation: Addressing the concern privately avoids public confrontation and allows the supervisor to handle the issue discreetly and effectively.

9. **C) Continue to monitor the situation and report any incidents** Explanation: Continuous monitoring ensures the behavior is addressed if it continues, protecting the team's safety and performance.

10. **B) To ensure the team's safety during emergencies**

    Explanation: Ensuring safety protocols are followed is essential to prevent accidents and injuries during real emergencies.

11. **B) Assess the structural integrity of the building**

    Explanation: Assessing the building's stability is crucial to ensure the safety of the rescuers and the trapped individuals before proceeding with rescue operations.

12. **A) Help them evacuate immediately**

    Explanation: Assisting people who need help ensures their safety and reduces the number of trapped individuals, allowing the team to focus on others.

13. **C) Call for backup and assist in freeing them**

    Explanation: Ensuring the trapped teammate is freed safely while calling for additional help is important to prevent further injury and maintain team integrity.

14. **B) Find an alternative route to reach them**

Explanation: Finding an alternative route ensures that the rescue can continue without delay, increasing the chances of reaching those in need.

15. **A) Evacuate everyone immediately**

Explanation: Immediate evacuation ensures the safety of all team members and victims, preventing additional casualties from the unstable building.

16. **C) Engage with the child and explain as much as possible** Explanation: Engaging with the child educates them about fire safety and encourages their interest, potentially inspiring future firefighters.

17. **A) Let them try it on under your supervision**

Explanation: Allowing the child to try on the helmet under supervision ensures their safety while fostering their curiosity and excitement.

18. **A) Provide general fire safety tips and offer to visit their home for a check**

Explanation: Offering detailed advice and a home visit ensures the parent receives accurate and practical fire safety information.

19. **B) Tell them to stop and explain the importance of the equipment**

Explanation: Educating the teenagers about the importance of the equipment ensures they understand the seriousness and prevents future misuse.

20. **A) Explain the steps to create a fire escape plan and provide a brochure**

Explanation: Providing clear, actionable advice and resources empowers the elderly person to create a fire escape plan, enhancing their safety.

21. **B) Stop using it and report the issue to your supervisor**

Explanation: Stopping use and reporting the issue ensures that the malfunctioning equipment is addressed promptly, preventing potential accidents.

22. **B) Inform another senior team member about the issue**

Explanation: Informing a senior team member ensures that the issue is addressed immediately, even if the supervisor is unavailable.

23. **B) Insist on reporting the issue and stop using the equipment**

Explanation: Insisting on following safety protocols and stopping use of the faulty equipment ensures the safety of everyone involved.

24. **B) Describe the malfunction in detail and its potential risks**

Explanation: Providing detailed information about the malfunction helps in understanding the severity of the issue and taking appropriate action.

25. **B) Suggest alternative training methods while the equipment is being repaired**

Explanation: Offering alternative methods ensures that training continues safely and without interruption.

26. **B) Offer to help them improve their fitness**

Explanation: Offering help and support promotes team cohesion and helps the new member improve, benefiting the entire team.

27. **B) Provide encouragement and offer personal training tips**

Explanation: Encouragement and personal tips help the new member feel supported and motivated to improve their performance.

28. **B) Allow a short break and offer to help them catch up**

Explanation: Allowing a break ensures the new member does not overexert themselves and can continue training effectively.

29. **A) Continue offering support and encouragement**

Explanation: Ongoing support and encouragement help the new member reach the required level without feeling abandoned.

30. **C) Publicly acknowledge their hard work**

Explanation: Public acknowledgment boosts morale and encourages continued improvement, benefiting the team.

31. **B) Assess the situation and prioritize the most critically injured**

Explanation: Prioritizing the most critically injured ensures that those who need immediate attention receive it, potentially saving lives.

32. **B) Apply pressure to stop the bleeding**

Explanation: Stopping severe bleeding is a critical first aid step that can save a person's life.

33. **B) Politely ask them to step back and let you work**

Explanation: Politely asking the bystander to step back allows you to focus on the victims without causing additional conflict.

34. **B) Use the appropriate tool to open the door**

Explanation: Using the right tool ensures the person is evacuated safely without causing further injury.

35. **B) Focus on rescuing them immediately**

Explanation: Immediate rescue of the trapped child ensures their safety and reduces their distress.

36. **B) Inform the business owner of the violations immediately**

Explanation: Informing the owner immediately ensures they are aware of the risks and can take prompt action to address them.

37. **B) Explain the importance of the changes for safety** Explanation: Explaining the importance of safety changes helps the owner understand the risks and the need for compliance.

38. **B) Inform the owner and ensure it is cleared immediately**

Explanation: Clearing the blocked emergency exit is crucial for safety, and informing the owner ensures they are aware of the issue.

39. **B) Inform the owner and recommend immediate replacement**

Explanation: Informing the owner about the expired extinguishers and recommending replacement ensures the business is prepared for emergencies.

40. **B) Schedule a follow-up inspection to ensure compliance**

Explanation: A follow-up inspection ensures that the business has addressed the safety violations, maintaining ongoing safety compliance.

41. **C) Evacuating the residents**

Explanation: Evacuating residents is the immediate priority to ensure their safety from the rapidly spreading wildfire.

42. **A) Go door-to-door to alert residents**

Explanation: Going door-to-door ensures that all residents are alerted and can evacuate safely.

43. **C) Explain the danger and strongly encourage them to leave**

Explanation: Explaining the danger and encouraging evacuation helps ensure the resident's safety without using force.

44. **B) Urge them to leave immediately without packing**

Explanation: Urging immediate evacuation ensures their safety from the approaching fire.

45. **A) Join the efforts to fight the fire**

Explanation: Joining the firefighting efforts after evacuation helps in controlling the fire and protecting the residential area.

46. **A) Check all equipment is in working order**

Explanation: Ensuring equipment is in working order before leaving guarantees readiness and effectiveness during the fire response.

47. **A) Set up the ladder truck to reach them**

Explanation: Setting up the ladder truck quickly provides a means to rescue people trapped on upper floors.

48. **B) Guide people to safer areas within the building**

Explanation: Guiding people to safer areas within the building helps prevent them from being exposed to smoke and other hazards.

49. **C) Enter the building to find another way to reach them**

Explanation: Finding an alternative route ensures the person is reached quickly, even if the primary ladder truck is unavailable.

50. **B) Continue evacuating people**

Explanation: Continuing evacuation ensures more people are brought to safety as the fire spreads.

51. **B) Calm them down and try to get them to respond**

Explanation: Calming the panicked team member helps them regain composure and ensures the safety of the team.

52. **B) Escort them out of the simulation area**

Explanation: Escorting them out ensures their safety and allows the exercise to continue without further disruption.

53. **A) Let them take over calming the panicked member**

Explanation: Allowing another team member to help ensures the panicked member receives attention while the exercise continues.

54. **D) Use calming techniques**

Explanation: Using calming techniques can help diffuse the situation and prevent it from escalating.

55. **B) Report the incident to the supervisor**

Explanation: Reporting the incident ensures the supervisor is aware and can take appropriate action, such as providing additional support.

56. **B) Explain the procedures to the staff and students beforehand**

Explanation: Explaining procedures ensures everyone knows what to do, making the drill more effective and less chaotic.

57. **B) Explain the importance of the drill and encourage participation**

Explanation: Encouraging participation helps students understand the seriousness of the drill and its importance for safety.

58. **B) Show them the route and explain in detail**

Explanation: Providing detailed instructions helps the teacher understand and effectively guide students during an actual emergency.

59. **B) Stop the drill and clarify roles**

Explanation: Clarifying roles ensures everyone knows their responsibilities, making the drill and future emergencies more efficient.

60. **B) Conduct a debriefing session to discuss what went well and what needs improvement**

Explanation: Debriefing helps identify areas for improvement and reinforces effective practices, enhancing overall safety.

61. **B) Listen to their concerns and provide specific advice**

Explanation: Listening and providing specific advice shows you are taking their concerns seriously and offering practical help.

62. **A) Advise them to contact local authorities**

Explanation: Contacting local authorities ensures the issue is addressed by those who can enforce safety regulations.

63. **B) Recommend they get one and provide tips on how to use it**

Explanation: Providing this advice helps them improve their personal safety and preparedness.

64. **A) Install smoke detectors in their apartment**

Explanation: Installing smoke detectors enhances their safety and compliance with fire safety regulations.

65. **B) Offer additional resources and contact information**

Explanation: Providing further resources ensures they have ongoing support and information to improve their safety.

66. **B) Assess the situation and identify the chemicals involved**

Explanation: Assessing the situation and identifying chemicals ensures appropriate safety measures are taken.

67. **D) Call for medical assistance**

Explanation: Ensuring medical assistance is on the way addresses the immediate health needs of the unconscious worker.

68. **B) Assist the team by providing information about the situation**

Explanation: Assisting the hazardous materials team with information ensures a coordinated and effective response.

69. **B) Use appropriate protective equipment and follow protocols**

Explanation: Following protocols and using protective gear ensures the safety of the rescuer and the trapped worker.

70. **B) Ensure all workers are accounted for and safe**

Explanation: Ensuring all workers are safe and accounted for is crucial after a rescue operation in a hazardous area.

71. **B) Instruct everyone to evacuate calmly and orderly**

Explanation: Instructing an orderly evacuation ensures everyone's safety and prevents panic.

72. **B) Guide them calmly and provide clear instructions**

Explanation: Providing clear instructions helps manage panic and ensures an effective evacuation.

73. **B) Assist them to the nearest exit**

Explanation: Assisting those struggling ensures their safety and helps maintain an orderly evacuation.

74. **B) Prevent re-entry and explain the safety risks**

Explanation: Preventing re-entry and explaining the risks ensures everyone's safety until the situation is confirmed safe.

75. **B) Conduct a debriefing session about the evacuation**

Explanation: Debriefing helps improve future evacuations and addresses any issues that arose during the false alarm.

76. **B) Evacuate residents from the area**

Explanation: Evacuating residents ensures their safety from the potentially explosive gas leak.

77. **B) Evacuate the building and call for the gas company**

Explanation: Evacuating and calling the gas company ensures the leak is addressed by professionals while keeping residents safe.

78. **B) Explain the danger and strongly encourage them to evacuate**

Explanation: Explaining the danger helps the resident understand the risk and encourages compliance.

79. **B) Evacuate immediately and warn others**

Explanation: Immediate evacuation prevents a potential explosion from causing harm.

80. **B) Conduct a safety check before allowing re-entry**

Explanation: A safety check ensures the area is safe before residents return, preventing further incidents.

81. **B) Provide detailed information on kitchen fire prevention tips**

Explanation: Providing detailed information educates the participant and helps prevent kitchen fires, enhancing community safety.

SPATIAL ORIENTATION ANSWER KEY

1: C) Behind

Explanation: If you are facing East, North is directly behind you.

2: A) East

Explanation: If a car is traveling South, its right side is facing West.

3: A) Left

Explanation: Turning left from facing West will make you face South.

4: A) West, then North

Explanation: To return to your starting point, you must walk West to undo the East steps and then North to undo the South steps.

5: A) West

Explanation: If you are facing North, West is to your left.

6: A) West

Explanation: If a train is moving North, West is to its left.

7: B) West

Explanation: Turning 90 degrees to the right from facing South will make you face West.

8: A) South, then East

Explanation: To return to your starting point, you must walk South to undo the North steps and then East to undo the West steps.

9: A) East

Explanation: If you are traveling West, East is directly behind you.

10: C) East

Explanation: If you are facing West, North is to your right.

11: A) West

Explanation: Turning left from facing North will make you face West.

12: A) West, then South

Explanation: To return to your starting point, you must walk West to undo the East steps and then South to undo the North steps.

13: A) South

Explanation: If a bus is traveling East, South is to its right.

14: A) West

Explanation: Turning 180 degrees from facing East will make you face West.

15: B) West, then North

Explanation: To return to your starting point, you must walk West to undo the South steps and then North to undo the East steps.

16: B) East

Explanation: If you are facing South, East is to your right.

17: A) North

Explanation: Turning right from facing West will make you face North.

18: A) South

Explanation: If a cyclist is traveling North, South is directly behind them.

19: A) South, then East

Explanation: To return to your starting point, you must walk South to undo the North steps and then East to undo the West steps.

20: C) West

Explanation: If you are facing East, North is to your left.

21: A) East

Explanation: Turning left from facing South will make you face East.

22: A) East

Explanation: If you are traveling North, East is directly to your right.

23: B) South, then West

Explanation: To return to your starting point, you must walk South to undo the North steps and then West to undo the East steps.

24: A) South

Explanation: Turning 90 degrees to the left from facing West will make you face South.

25: A) East

Explanation: If you are facing North, East is to your right.

26: A) South

Explanation: Turning right from facing East will make you face South.

27: A) North

Explanation: If you are traveling South, North is directly behind you.

28: A) North, then East

Explanation: To return to your starting point, you must walk North to undo the South steps and then East to undo the West steps.

29: A) North

Explanation: Turning 180 degrees from facing South will make you face North.

30: A) East

Explanation: If you are facing South, East is to your left.

31: A) North

Explanation: Turning left from facing East will make you face North.

32: A) West, then South

Explanation: To return to your starting point, you must walk West to undo the East steps and then South to undo the North steps.

33: A) West

Explanation: If you are facing East, West is directly behind you.

34: A) West

Explanation: Turning 90 degrees to the left from facing North will make you face West.

35: A) South

Explanation: If you are facing East, South is to your right.

36: A) North, then East

Explanation: To return to your starting point, you must walk North to undo the South steps and then East to undo the West steps.

37: A) West

Explanation: Turning right from facing South will make you face West.

38: A) West

Explanation: If you are traveling East, West is directly behind you.

39: A) South, then East

Explanation: To return to your starting point, you must walk South to undo the North steps and then East to undo the West steps.

40: A) East

Explanation: Turning 90 degrees to the right from facing North will make you face East.

41: A) South

Explanation: If you are facing West, South is to your left.

42: A) South

Explanation: Turning left from facing West will make you face South.

43: A) North, then West

Explanation: To return to your starting point, you must walk North to undo the South steps and then West to undo the East steps.

44: A) South

Explanation: If you are facing North, South is directly behind you.

45: A) East

Explanation: Turning 90 degrees to the left from facing South will make you face East.

46: A) West

Explanation: If you are facing South, West is to your right.

47: A) South, then West

Explanation: To return to your starting point, you must walk South to undo the North steps and then West to undo the East steps.

48: A) East

Explanation: Turning right from facing North will make you face East.

49: A) East

Explanation: If you are traveling West, East is directly behind you.

50: A) South, then West

Explanation: To return to your starting point, you must walk South to undo the North steps and then West to undo the East steps.

51: A) East

Explanation: Turning 180 degrees from facing West will make you face East.

52: A) North

Explanation: If you are facing East, North is to your left.

53: A) West

Explanation: Turning left from facing North will make you face West.

54: A) North, then West

Explanation: To return to your starting point, you must walk North to undo the South steps and then West to undo the East steps.

55: A) North

Explanation: If you are facing South, North is directly behind you.

56: A) South

Explanation: Turning 90 degrees to the right from facing East will make you face South.

57: A) North

Explanation: If you are facing West, North is to your right.

58: A) South, then West

Explanation: To return to your starting point, you must walk South to undo the North steps and then West to undo the East steps.

59: A) South

Explanation: Turning right from facing East will make you face South.

60: A) South Explanation: If you are traveling North, South is directly behind you.

61: A) North, then West

Explanation: To return to your starting point, you must walk North to undo the South steps and then West to undo the East steps.

62: A) East

Explanation: Turning 90 degrees to the left from facing South will make you face East.

63: A) West

Explanation: If you are facing North, West is to your left.

64: A) East

Explanation: Turning left from facing South will make you face East.

65: A) South, then West

Explanation: To return to your starting point, you must walk South to undo the North steps and then West to undo the East steps.

66: A) East

Explanation: If you are facing West, East is directly behind you.

67: A) North

Explanation: Turning 90 degrees to the left from facing East will make you face North.

68: A) South

Explanation: If you are facing East, South is to your right.

69: A) North, then East

Explanation: To return to your starting point, you must walk North to undo the South steps and then East to undo the West steps.

70: A) East

Explanation: Turning right from facing North will make you face East.

71: A) North

Explanation: If you are traveling South, North is directly behind you.

72: A) North, then West

Explanation: To return to your starting point, you must walk North to undo the South steps and then West to undo the East steps.

73: A) North

Explanation: Turning 90 degrees to the left from facing East will make you face North.

74: A) East

Explanation: If you are facing South, East is to your left.

75: A) South

Explanation: Turning left from facing West will make you face South.

76: A) West, then South

Explanation: To return to your starting point, you must walk West to undo the East steps and then South to undo the North steps.

77: A) West

Explanation: If you are facing East, West is directly behind you.

78: A) East

Explanation: Turning 90 degrees to the right from facing South will make you face East.

79: A) East

Explanation: If you are facing North, East is to your right.

80: A) North, then West

Explanation: To return to your starting point, you must walk North to undo the South steps and then West to undo the East steps.

81: A) West

Explanation: Turning right from facing South will make you face West.

CHAPTER 7

BONUS

30-Day Study Plan: Your Daily Prep Guide

Day 1: Start by familiarizing yourself with the exam format. Spend time reading through the study guide and any available materials about the structure of the exam. Note down important dates, requirements, and key topics. This foundational step will set the tone for your study plan.

Day 2: Begin with reading comprehension. Start with basic exercises that test your ability to understand and interpret passages. Focus on identifying main ideas, supporting details, and making inferences. Spend about two hours on this, followed by a short review session.

Day 3: Continue with reading comprehension, but increase the complexity of the passages. Practice summarizing paragraphs and answering questions related to the text. Review your answers and understand the rationale behind correct responses.

Day 4: Shift focus to mathematical reasoning. Begin with basic arithmetic and algebra. Work on problems involving addition, subtraction, multiplication, division, and simple algebraic equations. Spend a couple of hours practicing, followed by reviewing your solutions.

Day 5: Continue with mathematical reasoning, diving into geometry and statistics. Work on problems related to shapes, areas, volumes, and basic statistical concepts. Review any incorrect answers to understand your mistakes.

Day 6: Integrate mechanical reasoning into your study routine. Start with understanding basic mechanical principles such as levers, pulleys, and gears. Use visual aids and diagrams to help grasp these concepts. Practice solving related problems.

Day 7: Focus on situational judgment. Read scenarios and practice making decisions based on the information provided. Think about the implications of each choice and why it might be the best or worst option.

Day 8: Spend the day reviewing the topics covered in the first week. This includes reading comprehension, mathematical reasoning, mechanical reasoning, and situational judgment. Identify any weak areas and revisit them.

Day 9: Return to reading comprehension. This time, practice with longer passages and more complex questions. Work on your speed and accuracy. Try to simulate exam conditions by timing your practice sessions.

Day 10: Go back to mathematical reasoning. Focus on solving word problems that require a combination of arithmetic and algebra. Practice interpreting data from graphs and tables.

Day 11: Dive deeper into mechanical reasoning. Work on problems involving complex machines and their components. Understand the application of mechanical principles in real-world scenarios, particularly in firefighting contexts.

Day 12: Spend time on situational judgment exercises. Read through various scenarios and practice making quick, informed decisions. Discuss these scenarios with peers if possible to get different perspectives.

Day 13: Review the material covered in the past few days. Take practice quizzes on reading comprehension and mathematical reasoning. Identify patterns in the types of questions you find challenging and focus on those areas.

Day 14: Take a break from studying to rest and recharge. Use this day to relax, engage in physical activities, or do something enjoyable. Mental rest is crucial for effective learning.

Day 15: Start the second half of the study plan with a focus on practical skills. If possible, engage in hands-on activities related to mechanical reasoning, such as working with tools or building simple machines.

Day 16: Go back to reading comprehension. Practice with passages that cover technical and non-technical subjects. Focus on improving your ability to quickly grasp the main ideas and key details.

Day 17: Work on advanced mathematical reasoning problems. These could include more complex algebraic equations, geometry problems, and data analysis. Ensure you understand the underlying principles.

Day 18: Integrate situational judgment with practical scenarios. Think about real-life situations you might face as a firefighter and how you would handle them. Discuss these scenarios with colleagues or mentors.

Day 19: Spend the day reviewing all the topics. Take comprehensive practice tests that cover reading comprehension, mathematical reasoning, mechanical reasoning, and situational judgment. Review your answers thoroughly.

Day 20: Focus on the physical aspect of the firefighter exam. Incorporate physical training into your routine. Work on building stamina, strength, and agility. These physical skills are crucial for the practical components of the exam.

Day 21: Return to mechanical reasoning. Work on understanding how different mechanical systems operate. Practice identifying issues and troubleshooting problems in mechanical setups.

Day 22: Spend time on reading comprehension, focusing on specialized texts such as technical manuals or safety procedures. This will help you become comfortable with the type of reading material you might encounter in the field.

Day 23: Work on mathematical reasoning by solving problems that require critical thinking and application of multiple concepts. Practice with a variety of problem types to build versatility.

Day 24: Engage in situational judgment exercises that involve teamwork and leadership. Think about how you would lead a team during an emergency and the decisions you would need to make.

Day 25: Review the past week's material. Take practice exams under timed conditions to simulate the test environment. Focus on improving your speed and accuracy.

Day 26: Spend the day on hands-on practice. If possible, participate in training exercises or simulations that involve mechanical reasoning and situational judgment. Practical experience will reinforce your theoretical knowledge.

Day 27: Go back to reading comprehension. Practice with a focus on improving your ability to quickly scan and identify key information in long passages. Time yourself to improve your reading speed.

Day 28: Work on complex mathematical reasoning problems. These should challenge your understanding and push you to apply multiple concepts to find solutions. Review any mistakes to understand where you went wrong.

Day 29: Spend the day reviewing all the material. Take a comprehensive practice test that includes all sections of the exam. Identify any last-minute weak areas and focus on them.

Day 30: Rest and relax. Avoid any intense studying. Go over your notes lightly and ensure you have everything you need for the exam day. Engage in light physical activity to keep your body and mind fresh.

This 30-day study plan is designed to provide a balanced and comprehensive approach to preparing for the firefighter exam. Each day focuses on different aspects of the exam, ensuring that you build a strong foundation in all areas.

Regular review sessions and practical exercises will help reinforce your knowledge and improve your confidence. By following this plan, you'll be well-prepared to tackle the exam and take the first step towards a rewarding career as a firefighter.

Test Day Strategies: Peak Performance When It Counts

On the day of an important exam, like the firefighter exam, performance isn't just about how much you've studied; it's also about how you approach the test itself. Implementing effective test day strategies can greatly enhance your ability to perform under pressure and can help ensure that all your hard work pays off. Here are some tips designed to maximize your performance when it really counts.

The night before the exam is crucial. Ensure you have everything prepared well in advance—this includes gathering all necessary documentation, such as identification and admission tickets, and checking your supplies. Make sure you have several pencils, a sharpener, an eraser, a calculator if allowed, and any other allowable resources. This preparation helps minimize stress on the actual day, allowing you to focus solely on the task at hand.

Sleep is your best friend when it comes to high-stakes testing. The night before the exam, try to get at least 7-8 hours of excellent quality sleep. A well-rested brain performs significantly better in terms of memory recall and logical reasoning, both of which are crucial for a firefighter exam that tests both your academic and practical knowledge.

On the morning of the exam, follow a routine that sets a positive tone for the day. This might involve exercise, a hearty breakfast, and a review of your notes. Physical activity can boost your endorphins, which improves mood and reduces stress. A hearty meal gives you the energy you need to concentrate during a long exam. However, avoid heavy and unfamiliar foods that might upset your stomach. Reviewing notes should be light; this is not the time for cramming but rather a moment for reinforcing key concepts already learned.

Arriving early at the exam venue can provide you with several advantages. It allows you time to adapt to the testing environment, reduces anxiety about being late, and gives you a few moments to calm your nerves. Use this time to practice breathing exercises or positive visualizations to enhance your focus and ease any lingering anxiety.

During the exam, it's important to read each question carefully. Under the stress of a timed test, many candidates rush through the instructions or the questions and make careless mistakes. Take your time to understand what each question is asking. If you don't know the answer immediately, move on to the next question. It's better to leave a question temporarily unanswered than to spend too much time on it and not have the opportunity to answer questions that you might know.

Managing your time efficiently is another crucial test-taking strategy. Be aware of the time, but don't be ruled by it. If the exam allows, tackle the easier questions first to build your confidence and ensure you secure those marks without spending too much time pondering the more challenging ones. Then, return to the more difficult questions with any remaining time. This approach maximizes your scoring potential.

If you feel overwhelmed at any point, pause for a moment. Close your eyes, take a few deep breaths, and refocus. Remember, it's entirely normal to feel a bit anxious during an exam; what's important is how you handle that anxiety. Re-centering your thoughts can help prevent them from spiraling and keep you on track.

It's also helpful to simulate real exam conditions when you practice. This includes timing your practice sessions and sitting in a chair at a desk, which replicates the setup you'll face on test day. The more accustomed you are to the conditions, the less intimidating the exam will feel.

Lastly, maintain a positive attitude throughout the preparation and execution of the exam. Confidence is built not just from mastering the subject matter but also from mastering your mindset. Believe in your preparation, trust in your abilities, and maintain a mindset that you are going to perform to the best of your capabilities.

By following these test-day strategies, you ensure that you are not just well-prepared in terms of study but also ready to tackle the exam environment itself. Each tip is designed to optimize your performance, reduce test-day anxiety, and enable you to demonstrate your true capabilities. Remember, it's not just what you know; it's also how you apply it under pressure that counts.

Physical Test Tips: Preparing Your Body for the Challenge

Preparing your body for the physical demands of a firefighting test is as crucial as the intellectual preparation for the written exam. Firefighting is a physically demanding job that requires not only mental acuity but also a high level of physical fitness. Here's how you can prepare your body for the challenge ahead, ensuring that you are as physically equipped as possible to meet the demands of the test.

Physical fitness for firefighting encompasses various aspects of physical health, including strength, endurance, agility, and flexibility. Every one of these elements is essential to a firefighter's capacity to work well under duress, manage the physical demands of the work, and lower their risk of injury.

To begin with, strength training is fundamental. Firefighters must often carry heavy equipment, break down doors, or even carry individuals to safety. To develop the required muscle strength, include a weight training program that emphasizes compound movements like bench presses, deadlifts, and squats. It's important to focus on building strength in both the upper and lower body. Exercises like pull-ups, rows, and leg presses are also crucial. These exercises not only increase muscle mass but also improve your overall body strength, which is essential for the physical tasks firefighters perform on the job.

Endurance training is another critical component. A firefighter must be able to perform strenuously over extended periods. Cardiovascular fitness can be enhanced through activities such as running, swimming, or cycling. High-intensity interval training (HIIT) can also be extremely beneficial as it mimics the burst of intense physical activity followed by periods of rest, which is typical in firefighting scenarios. Training for endurance will help ensure that your heart and lungs are conditioned to handle prolonged physical activity without fatigue setting in too quickly.

Agility and flexibility may not immediately seem as critical as strength and endurance, but being agile allows a firefighter to navigate challenging environments swiftly and safely. Drills that enhance agility, such as ladder runs, cone drills, and short sprints that require quick changes of direction, can be very beneficial. Flexibility exercises, including dynamic stretching before workouts and static stretching afterward, help improve the range of motion and decrease the risk of injuries. Enhancing flexibility and core strength is essential for properly lifting and moving heavy equipment, and yoga and pilates are great for this.

Consistency in your training regimen is key. Ideally, a mix of strength, endurance, and flexibility training should be part of your weekly routine. Plan to exercise at least four to five days per week, with a combination of strength training and cardiovascular workouts. Rest days are also vital to allow your muscles time to recover and grow stronger. The body's capacity to function might be compromised, and injury risk might escalate in the absence of sufficient rest.

Hydration and nutrition are essential for physical fitness. The energy required for intense training and recuperation is provided by a well-balanced diet high in proteins, carbs, and healthy fats. Equally crucial is staying hydrated, particularly during extended and strenuous workout sessions. In addition to lubricating joints and helping to carry minerals for energy production and overall health, water also helps control body temperature. Throughout the day, remember to stay hydrated, especially before, during, and after physical activity.

It is important to include mental preparation in addition to physical exercise. It needs both mental and physical power to be able to remain composed under duress, stay focused for extended periods of time, and finish physically taxing tasks. Mental resilience can be improved by using techniques like visualization, in which you picture yourself accomplishing physical activities effectively. Additionally helpful in reducing stress and enhancing focus are mindfulness and meditation.

In the weeks leading up to the test, it's wise to simulate the test conditions as closely as possible. If you know the specific activities that will be part of the test, practice these repeatedly. For example, if the test includes carrying a weighted pack, training by walking, or running with a weighted backpack to acclimate your body to the strain. If ladder climbs are part of the test, include ladder drills in your routine. This not only prepares your body for specific challenges but also helps build confidence.

As test day approaches, taper your training to avoid burnout or injuries. Reduce the intensity and volume of workouts to ensure your body is well-rested and at peak performance on test day.

Lastly, remember that the journey to becoming a firefighter is a marathon, not a sprint. Building physical fitness takes time, dedication, and perseverance. Each day that you train, you are not only preparing to pass a physical test but also preparing to take on one of the most demanding and rewarding careers. Physical readiness ensures you have the strength and stamina to save lives, protect property, and handle the rigorous duties of firefighting with competence and courage.

Managing Stress Before, During, and After the Exam

Managing stress related to the exam process is crucial for maximizing performance and maintaining mental health. Stress can be a significant barrier to success, affecting concentration, memory, and overall ability to perform under pressure. To make sure you stay calm and concentrate the entire exam, you must learn stress management techniques before, during, and after the exam.

Before the exam, it's important to establish a routine that includes regular study breaks and time for relaxation. Dedicating moments for activities that you enjoy, such as reading, walking, or listening to music, can greatly reduce pre-exam anxiety. Additionally, maintaining a consistent sleep schedule that allows for adequate rest each night can help mitigate stress and improve cognitive function.

Visualization techniques are particularly effective for managing stress. Before the exam, spend time visualizing a successful exam experience. Picture yourself calmly reading through the questions, confidently writing the answers, and feeling prepared and in control. This mental rehearsal can enhance your self-confidence and reduce anxiety.

If you experience feelings of overload during the exam, take a few moments to concentrate on deep breathing. In addition to promoting calmness, controlled breathing improves brain oxygen flow, which improves cognitive function. Prior to the exam, it can be beneficial to practice mindfulness meditation since this can help you learn how to remain focused and present under pressure.

After the exam, it's important to decompress and disconnect from the intensity of the study schedule. Engage in social activities, spend time outdoors, or pursue hobbies that you had to set aside during your preparation. Reflecting on what you've learned and how you've developed can also be a source of satisfaction and can reduce post-exam stress.

Recognizing that stress is a normal part of the exam process and having strategies in place to manage it will not only help you during the test but will also benefit you in various high-pressure situations throughout your career. Embracing these techniques ensures that you handle the exam efficiently and maintain your well-being throughout the process.

Career Path and Advancement Advice

Navigating the career path and seeking advancement in the field of firefighting requires a proactive approach and a clear understanding of the opportunities and challenges that lie ahead. The journey from entry-level firefighter to a leadership position such as captain, chief, or even specialized roles like fire investigator or fire safety educator involves continuous learning, experience, and personal development.

One of the first steps in advancing your firefighting career is to gain a solid foundation through on-the-job experience. Every call and response provides a learning opportunity, whether it involves combating fires, conducting rescues, or engaging in community safety education. It's important to be observant, ask questions, and learn from more experienced colleagues. Demonstrating reliability, decision-making skills, and a commitment to team success are essential traits that help in gaining recognition and eligibility for promotions.

Education also plays a critical role in career advancement. Many firefighters choose to pursue further education in fire science, emergency management, or public administration. These programs offer deeper insights into fire behavior, building codes, arson investigation, and the management of emergency services. Higher education not only broadens your knowledge but also makes you a more competitive candidate for higher positions that require advanced skills and understanding.

Certifications are another key element in advancing within the fire service. Specialized training programs such as EMT or paramedic certification, hazardous materials handling, and rescue operations can open doors to new roles within the department. These certifications increase your versatility and value to the team, often leading to more responsibilities and higher pay.

Networking and mentorship are invaluable in this progression. Building relationships with peers and superiors can provide support, advice, and information about opportunities for advancement. Mentors can assist you in negotiating the challenges of developing a career in firefighting by providing advice based on their own experiences.

Finally, leadership skills are crucial for advancement in the firefighting career. As you move up the ranks, the ability to lead effectively becomes increasingly important. Leadership in firefighting isn't just about directing others; it also involves strategy, crisis management, and the ability to inspire and maintain team morale under stressful conditions. Engaging in leadership training workshops and taking on leadership roles, even in small capacities, can prepare you for future positions of greater responsibility.

By combining experience, education, certification, networking, and leadership development, you can strategically navigate the path to career advancement in firefighting. Each step taken is not just about climbing the ranks but also about becoming a more skilled and knowledgeable professional who can significantly contribute to the safety and well-being of the community.

CONCLUSION

Encouragement to embrace the challenges and rewards of a firefighting career

Embracing a career in firefighting is not just about choosing a job; it's about committing to a lifestyle of courage, dedication, and service. Firefighters are revered in society not only because they fight fires and save lives but also because they embody the spirit of community service and heroism. This career, filled with challenges and risks, is also immensely rewarding, offering a unique opportunity to make a substantial impact on people's safety and lives daily.

Firefighting is a profession that calls for physical bravery and mental strength. Every day, firefighters face unpredictable environments, and their actions directly contribute to preventing tragedies and alleviating distress. However, the essence of firefighting transcends the immediate rush of adrenaline. It's about the profound satisfaction of knowing that every day at work is an opportunity to protect lives and properties, educate people about fire safety, and be a comforting presence in the worst of times.

Moreover, firefighting fosters a sense of brotherhood and camaraderie rarely found in other professions. The bonds formed between firefighters are forged in the heat of shared challenges, relying on each other unequivocally in life-threatening situations. This creates a deep-seated sense of belonging and loyalty, contributing to a fulfilling work environment where each member uplifts and supports one another.

The path of a firefighter is also one of continuous learning and personal growth. The profession demands constant physical training, learning new firefighting techniques, and adapting to the latest technologies and methods. There is always room for improvement and advancement, making it a career that never stagnates. As you grow in your role, you gain not just ranks but also respect, knowledge, and the ability to influence positive changes within your community.

For those who aspire to make a difference, firefighting offers a direct route to impactful service. It is a career that calls for selflessness, resilience, and an unwavering commitment to safeguarding others. Every challenge faced is an opportunity to display courage, and every call answered is a chance to enhance the safety and well-being of individuals directly.

As you consider or continue on the path to becoming a firefighter, let the scale of the impact you can have fuel your journey. Embrace each challenge as an opportunity to demonstrate strength, and let each reward remind you of the vital role you play. The road is demanding, but the sense of fulfillment derived from serving others and saving lives is unparalleled. The firefighting community awaits with open arms, ready to welcome those brave enough to step forward and stand among those who choose daily to make a heroic difference.

Thank you for completing our Firefighter Exam Prep Guide. We trust that the information and tips provided have prepared you for successfully passing the firefighter exam. Your journey through this guide is a significant step toward a rewarding career in firefighting. Please take a moment to leave a review on Amazon and let us know how this guide has helped you. Your experiences and insights are crucial for us and help future readers gain the most from their preparation.

How You Can Share Your Review:

Through Amazon.com:

1. Go to the Amazon page where you found my book.
2. Navigate to the 'Customer Reviews' section.
3. Click on 'Write a customer review' to share your valuable insights.

Instant QR Code Access: Simply scan the QR code below with your smartphone to be directed to the Amazon review section.

Made in United States
Orlando, FL
13 September 2024